MINUTE
GUIDE TO
WordPerfect
Presentations

Michael Griffin

alpha
books

A Division of Macmillan Computer Publishing
201 West 103rd Street, Indianapolis, Indiana 46290 USA

©1994 Alpha Books

International Standard Book Number: 1-56761-537-6
Library of Congress Catalog Card Number: 94-78721

96 95 94   8 7 6 5 4 3 2 1

Interpretation of the printing code: the rightmost number of the first series of numbers is the year of the book's printing; the rightmost number of the second series of numbers is the number of the book's printing. For example, a printing code of 94-1 shows that the first printing of the book was in 1994.

Screen reproductions in this book were created by means of the program Collage Plus from Inner Media, Inc., Hollis, NH.

Printed in the United States of America

Publisher: Marie Butler-Knight
Managing Editor: Elizabeth Keaffaber
Development Editor: Melanie Palaisa
Production Editor: Phil Kitchel
Copy Editor: San Dee Philips
Book Designer: Barbara Kordesh
Cover Design: Dan Armstrong
Indexer: Johnna VanHoose
Production: Gary Adair, Dan Caparo, Brad Chinn, Kim Cofer, David Dean, Lisa Daugherty, Cynthia Drouin, David Eason, Jennifer Eberhardt, Erica Millen, Beth Rago, Bobbi Satterfield, Michael Thomas, Karen Walsh, Robert Wolf

Special thanks to Herb Felther for ensuring the technical accuracy of this book.

Contents

Introduction

WP Presentations is a powerful and easy-to-use presentations program. You can use it to quickly create and modify slide show presentations and create speaker notes to guide you through your oral presentation. Now that you have the program, where do you begin? Well, you're off to the right start with the *10 Minute Guide to WordPerfect Presentations*. This book will help you learn the program quickly and learn only the information necessary to perform specific tasks.

What Is a 10 Minute Guide?

The *10 Minute Guide* series is an efficient approach to learning computer programs. Like all *10 Minute Guides*, this one consists of over 20 lessons, each designed to be completed in 10 minutes or less. These lessons contain clear-cut, straight-to-the-point instructions. We have attempted to write the book in plain English—taking care to avoid computer jargon. Each lesson is a self-contained series of steps that teaches you how to perform a specific task.

What Is WP Presentations?

WP Presentations is a slide show program, also called *presentations software*. This software allows you to create impressive presentations in an easy and efficient manner. With its paint/draw/text tools, you can create slide shows in a snap. Two other important time-saving features of the software are the Outliner and the Master Gallery. The Outliner lets you organize your notes and information into a traditional outline format. The Master Gallery lets you choose from many ready-made slide backgrounds upon which you can enter your notes, charts, and artwork.

WP Presentations also provides a variety of slide templates to help you present a variety of information: from organization charts, to statistical charts, such as bar and pie charts and graphs, to simple bulleted lists and paragraphs.

WP Presentations provides a lot of flexibility in the type of artwork and graphics you can create, import, or link into your slide show. You can add music and sounds to your slide show using MIDI (musical digital interface), digital audio, and compact disc (CDs) capabilities.

With WP Presentations you can display your slide show on your computer screen, project it on a movie screen like a traditional slide show (assuming you have an overhead projector that works with your PC), or save the slide show in a file format (such as TIFF, PCX, and so on) that will allow a slide show service bureau to create 35mm slides for a slide projector.

Conventions Used in This Book

Each lesson in this book is set up in an easily accessible and consistent format. Steps that you perform are numbered. Pictures of screens show you what to expect. And the following icons point out definitions, warnings, and tips to help you understand what you're doing and stay out of trouble.

Plain English icons define new terms.

Panic Button icons appear where new users commonly run into trouble.

Timesaver Tips offer shortcuts and hints for using the program effectively.

In addition, here are a few more conventions that will help you:

What you type	Information you type appears in bold, blue type.
On-screen text	Text that appears on the screen appears in bold type.
Press Enter	Keys you press (or selections you make with the mouse) appear in blue type.

How to Use This Book

If you haven't installed WP Presentations, turn to the inside cover of this book for installation instructions. With the software installed, you can begin learning. Think of this book as a basic course on WP Presentations. Begin with Lesson 1 and work through to the end of the book. Or if you prefer, you can skip to any lesson to learn the WP Presentations feature you are most interested in. You can also use this *10 Minute Guide* as a quick reference; keep it nearby to learn how to perform a specific task.

If you are a new Windows user and would like a quick lesson on the basics of Windows, work through the Appendix, the "Microsoft Windows Primer." It covers how to start Windows, how to use the mouse, and how to navigate through Windows.

Trademarks

All terms mentioned in this book that are known to be trademarks have been appropriately capitalized. Alpha Books cannot attest to the accuracy of this information. Use of a term in this book should not be regarded as affecting the validity of any trademark or service mark.

Lesson

Starting and Exiting WordPerfect Presentations

In this lesson, you will learn how to start WordPerfect Presentations so that you can begin creating slide shows. You will also learn how to exit and get Help when you need it.

Starting WordPerfect Presentations

If you're familiar with Microsoft Windows, you already know how to start WordPerfect Presentations. In Windows, you start a program by double-clicking on its icon. To start Presentations, perform these steps:

1. Start Windows by typing **win** at the **C:>** prompt. The Windows Program Manager appears.

2. If the Presentations program group does not appear, click on Window in the menu bar and select WP Presentations. You can also click on the Word-Perfect Presentations group icon.

3. Double-click on the WP Presentations icon, as shown in Figure 1.1. The Presentations program starts. The first time you start the program, the License Number dialog box appears. Enter the license number found on your Certificate of License, and click on the OK button.

Double-click on this icon
to start the program.

The WordPerfect Presentations
program group window.

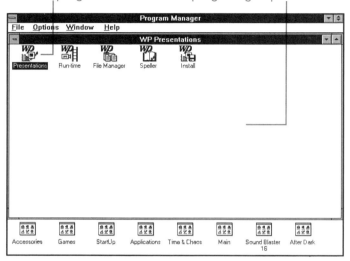

Figure 1.1 Double-click on the WordPerfect Presentations
icon to start the program.

Getting Help

If you don't know how to use a feature or perform a task,
Presentations offers several help features that can show you
how to perform basic and advanced tasks. One way to get
help is to click on the Help menu and select Contents. A
Help window appears with a series of buttons across the top
of the screen.

Contents   Displays a list of Help features.

Search   Displays an alphabetical list of Help topics
and lets you search for a Help topic using keywords.

Back   Returns you to the previous Help window.

History   Displays a list of the Help topics you have recently reviewed.

Print   Prints the current Help window.

<<   Goes back to a previous Help screen in a related series of Help screens.

>>   Goes forward to the next Help screen in a related series of Help screens.

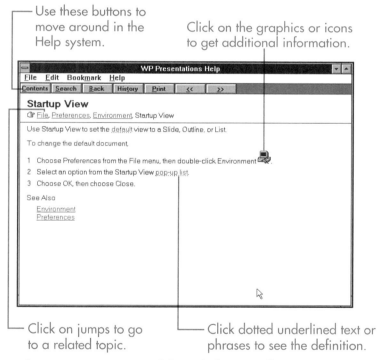

Use these buttons to move around in the Help system.

Click on the graphics or icons to get additional information.

Click on jumps to go to a related topic.

Click dotted underlined text or phrases to see the definition.

Figure 1.2   Jumps and the Help buttons allow you to move through the Help system.

In many of the Help windows, you will find *jumps*: graphics or underlined green words or phrases that you can click on to go to another Help topic (see Figure 1.2). In addition to jumps, you can click on important terms that are underlined with a dotted line, and a definition of that term will pop up in a window.

While trying to perform tasks in Presentations, you can also use two other features to get help:

Context-sensitive help   You can get help at any time by pressing F1. If you are in a dialog box, menu, or window and you need help, press F1 and Presentations will help you with the task you are trying to perform.

Help buttons   Some dialog boxes contain Help buttons that will also provide helpful information explaining the dialog box or the command you are trying to execute.

Dialog Box   A small window that allows you to select options by choosing command buttons. When you select many menu items, dialog boxes will appear. Some dialog boxes also display warnings and information messages you need to consider before taking action.

Using Search to Get Help

You may sometimes want more information on a particular feature, or simply need a definition of a term. Use the Search button to find topics by feature name or keyword, by following these steps:

1. Click on the Help menu.

2. Click on Search for Help on. The Search dialog box appears, as shown in Figure 1.3.

3. Type the word or phrase you want to search for in the text box, or select a word or phrase from the list box.

Enter word or
phrase here.

You also can
select a topic
from here.

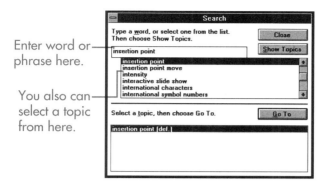

Figure 1.3   Searching for a topic.

4. Double-click on a term from the list of terms. You
can also click on the Show Topics button or press
Enter.

5. Double-click on a term from the list of topics. You
can also select the topic you want to view, and click
on the Go To button. A window with the topic you
selected appears.

Exiting Presentations

When you finish working with Presentations, choose any of
the following three ways to exit the program.

- Open the File menu and click on Exit.

- Press Alt+F4.

- Double-click on the Presentations Control-menu
box (the small box at the upper left corner of the
screen).

In this lesson, you learned how to start Presentations
and how to exit when you finish. You also learned some
basics about the on-line Help system. In the next lesson, you
will learn how to move around in Presentations, setting the
stage for your first slide-show creation.

Lesson

Moving Around in the Presentations Window

In this lesson, you will learn about the basic layout of the WP Presentations window, some Button Bar and tool palette basics, and how to change default settings.

A Look at the Presentations Window

The WP Presentations window contains many of the same elements you find in other Windows programs, such as drop-down menus, icons, buttons, and other features that make it easy and intuitive to use. Figure 2.1 shows the basic elements of the WP Presentations window. At the heart of the application window is the document window. This is where you do your work, creating drawings, charts, figures, lists, and outlines for your slide show.

Application Window The application window contains the operating features of WP Presentations, such as the menu bar, Button Bar, and tool palette. Inside the application window, you see another window: the document or drawing window.

Plain English

Figure 2.1   The WP Presentations window.

Here is a list of some of the important elements of the WP
Presentations Window and a brief explanation of each.

Title bar   Located at the very top of the WP Presentations window showing the name of the program and
the name of the slide show.

Menu bar   Located under the title bar, containing
the menu titles for topics, such as File, Edit, and View.
To find out what commands are available under each
topic, click on the menu title and a drop-down menu
will appear.

Button Bar   Located below the menu bar with
buttons that allow you to do several different things
with your slide show. You can quickly execute menu

commands, such as opening and closing slides, drawing graphics, changing text, and many others (see Lesson 20). To execute any of the tasks represented by a button, click the button. When you first open WP Presentations, the Button Bar will not be displayed. Learn how to display the Button Bar later in this lesson.

Tool palette   The tool palette (see Figure 2.2) is a rectangular area of the screen located on the left side of the Presentations window containing small icons called *tools*, which you can use to add, change, or enhance text and graphics in the slide show you have displayed. To use a tool, click on the icon that represents the tool.

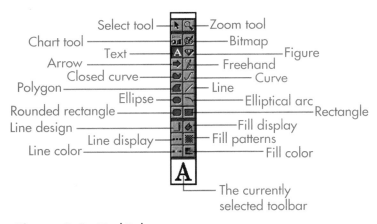

Figure 2.2   Tool Palette.

Slide scroll bar   Located at the bottom of the Presentations window, you can use the slide scroll bar when you want to move from one slide to another. Click the right arrow of the slide scroll bar to move ahead one slide or click the left arrow to move back one slide.

Template button   Located at the bottom right of the
Presentations window, you can click on the Template
button to display a list of slide layouts, charts, and
backgrounds that you can build upon to create your
slide shows.

Slide Show View buttons   Located at the bottom of
the screen, you can click on these buttons to get one
of four different views of your slide show. You can
click the first button from the left to display the Slide
Editor view. This view shows you individual slides.
The second button is the Outliner button that shows a
slide show in a text outline format. The third button
from the left displays the slide show list. The list
contains the numbers and titles of the slides and other
slide information. Click on the last button to display
the Slide Show Sorter; an overview of the slide show.
The Slide Show Sorter shows small sketches of each
slide, and you can use it to change the order of the
slides.

Control-menu box   Contains the commands (Restore, Move, Size, and so on) that allow you to control
the size and position of the WP Presentations window.
All Windows programs have a Control-menu box that
functions the same way.

Minimize button   Click to shrink the WP Presentations window down to an icon (small picture). All
Windows programs have a Maximize button that
functions the same way.

Restore button   Click to bring the WP Presentations
slide window back to its previous size.

Button Bar Basics

The Button Bar is a time-saving feature that lets you perform a task with a click of a button rather than executing multiple step commands from the menu bar or the tool palette. You can position the Button Bar at the top, left, right, or bottom of the screen. You can also create your own "customized" Button Bars to include the commands you use most. These features are discussed in Lesson 19, "Working with Button Bars."

Displaying the Button Bar

The initial default setting for WP Presentations is to hide, or not display, the Button Bar. However, since the Button Bar is such a helpful feature, you probably will display it while working in WP Presentations. To display the Button Bar, follow these steps:

1. Open the View menu, and click on Button Bar. The first time you do this, WP Presentations displays the Button Bar.

Changing the Button Bar

If the main Button Bar doesn't have the features you want to use while working on your slide show, you can choose features and commands from eleven other predefined Button Bars.

Here are the eleven predefined Button Bars and a brief description of each:

Table 2.1 Predefined Button Bars That You Can Choose

Button Bar	Helps You To...
drawing.prb	Draw shapes on your slides.
editing.prb	Edit.

Button Bar	Helps You To...
learn.prb	Run the tutorials of the *WP Presentations Lessons* guide that comes with the software.
prdatcht.prb	Work with charts.
prmain.prb	Choose basic commands, such as Open, Save, Print, and Exit.
prpaint.prb	Create graphic images.
prtxtcht.prb	Work with organization charts and bulleted list charts.
slide.prb	Create a slide.
slideshw.prb	Create a slide show.
text.prb	Create and edit text in a text box on a slide.
wp{pr}.prb	Use common commands and features, such as Open, Save, Print, and Play Slide Show. This is the default Button Bar that first appears.

To select the Button Bar you want to display, follow these steps:

1. Open the View menu, click on Button Bar Setup, and click on Select. The Select Button Bar dialog box appears, as is shown in Figure 2.3.

2. Specify the Button Bar you want by highlighting the Button Bar file name in the Files list box.

3. Click on the Select button. The Button Bar will appear.

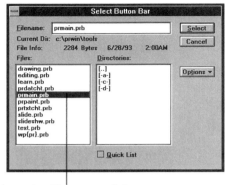

Click on the file name of the Button
Bar that you want to display.

Figure 2.3 Selecting a Button Bar to display.

In this lesson, you learned some basic features of the
WP Presentations window and the basics of how to display
and use the Button Bar. In the next lesson, you can use your
knowledge of the WP Presentations window to begin creating a slide show.

Lesson

Creating a New Slide Show

3

In this lesson, you will learn how to work with slide show masters and templates, and how to add and delete slides to create a slide show.

Choosing a Slide Show Master

Your first step in creating a slide show is to choose a slide design called a *slide show master*. Masters bring a consistent and professional look to your slide show. A slide show master provides a background design and color that will serve as the backdrop or foundation for every slide in your entire slide show. For example, if you choose the master slide called City, each slide in your slide show will have a city skyline in the background. As you will see, there are many slide show masters from which you can choose the one that is best suited for the information you want to present. To choose a slide show master, perform the following steps:

1. Open the Slide menu, and click on Master Gallery. The Master Gallery dialog box appears displaying a small sketch of each slide show master, as shown in Figure 3.1

2. Use the scroll bars to see the entire selection of slide masters. Click on the sketch of the master you want. A broken-lined box will appear around the selected master sketch.

Sketch of each
slide show master

Scroll bar

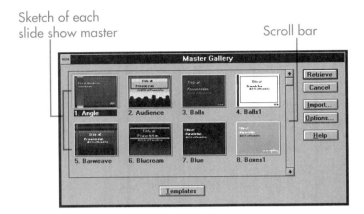

Figure 3.1   The Master Gallery dialog box.

3. Click on the Retrieve button and the master will
appear as your first slide.

Blank Slide   If, after you click on the Retrieve
button, your first slide comes up blank or white,
your slide is set to the No Template template. See
the next section, "Choosing a Template," to learn
how to fix this problem.

Choosing a Template

Now that you have chosen a slide show master for your
background, you can select a template to help you structure
and organize your information. *Templates* are commonly
used, generic slide designs that aid you in laying out and
organizing the information you want to present on each
slide. Templates ensure that you don't put too much or too
little information on each slide, and that the final slide looks
"balanced" in its appearance. Unlike the slide show master,
you can apply a different template to each slide in the slide
show. For example, one slide may be an organization chart,

one may be a bulleted list, and another may be a bar chart. Templates are time-savers. If you need to create an organization chart, you don't have to draw lines and boxes; the Presentations template will do that for you. To choose a template for your slide show master, perform the following steps:

1. Open the Slide menu, and click on Template. The Slide Template dialog box appears as shown in Figure 3.2.

To apply a template to a particular slide, click on these arrows.

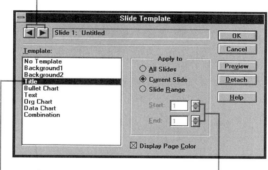

Click on a template name.   For applying a template to a range of slides, you can use these arrow buttons or enter the range numbers in the Start and End text boxes.

Figure 3.2   The Slide Template dialog box.

2. Click on the right or left arrow buttons at the top of the Slide Template dialog box to specify the slide number you want the template to apply to. If you want to apply the template to selected slides, click one of the following option buttons:

All Slides   Applies the template design to all slides in your slide show.

Current Slide   Applies the template design to the slide that is currently on display in your slide show.

Slide Range   Applies the template design to a range of slides in the show, such as slides 7 through 16. If you click on Slide Range, you must also specify the range by entering a starting slide number and an ending slide number in the range boxes or by clicking the arrow buttons that are next to the range boxes.

3. Click on the template you want from the Template list box. The choices are:

No Template   Provides a blank slide with a white background. You will not see the slide show master when you choose this template.

Background 1   When you select a slide show master, you can change the layout of the pictures or designs in that master slightly by choosing the Background 1 template. It will provide a slightly different look to your master.

Background 2   When you select a slide show master, you can change the layout of the pictures or designs in that master slightly by choosing the Background 2 template. It will provide a slightly different look to your master.

Title   Provides a predesigned slide that you can use as the first slide of the show. This template formats the main title and subtitles of the overall slide show.

Bullet Chart   Provides a predesigned title slide with a format for listing your most important points in a prominent display and your secondary points in an indented display.

Text   Provides a predesigned title slide formatted so that you can enter a paragraph of text.

Org Chart   Provides a predesigned title slide and a generic organizational-chart format that you can change to fit your personnel organization.

Data Chart   Provides a predesigned data-based chart, such as a line, bar, or pie chart.

Data-Based Chart   You can create a data-based chart from numbers that you enter into a worksheet. WP Presentations has the capability of automatically creating a chart from the information you enter in rows and columns on the worksheet area.

Combination   Provides a predesigned template that is a combination of a data chart and a title slide.

4. Click on the Preview button to view the template you have highlighted. A smaller window appears on the screen to give you a sketch of the template.

5. Click on the OK button. WP Presentation applies the template design you selected to the selected slide or slides.

Shortcut   You also can click on the Template pop-up list button at the bottom of the Presentations window to select a template for the current master. When you click on the Template Pop-up List button, hold down the mouse button to keep the list of templates open so you can highlight your choice.

Adding a Slide

You can add a slide (which is nothing more than a new window onto which you can add text or pictures) or a group of slides to your slide show at any time. To add a slide, perform these steps:

1. Open the Slide menu, and click on Add Slide. The Add Slide dialog box appears as shown in Figure 3.3.

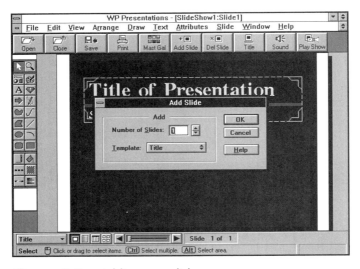

Figure 3.3   Adding new slides.

2. Enter the number of slides you want to add in the Number of Slides text box, or specify the number by clicking the up or down arrow button to increase or decrease the number of slides to be added to the show.

3. Click and hold the mouse button on the Template Pop-up List button to select the template you want to apply to the new slides. If you don't select a template to apply to the new slides, the template from the current slide will automatically be applied to the new slides.

4. Click on the OK button. WP Presentation adds the new slide or slides to the slide show.

> **Shortcut Keys**   You can quickly add a slide by pressing the shortcut key combination Ctrl+Enter.

Deleting a Slide

You can delete a slide from your slide show at any time. To delete a slide, perform the following steps:

1. Click the left or right Slide scroll bar arrows at the bottom of the screen to display the slide you want to delete.

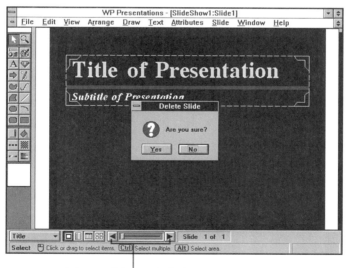

Slide scroll bar. Click the arrows to find the slide you want to delete.

Figure 3.4   The Delete Slide dialog box and the Slide scroll bar.

2. Open the Slide menu, and click on Delete Slide. The Delete Slide dialog box appears allowing you to confirm that you want to delete the current slide (see Figure 3.4).

3. Click Yes to delete the selected slide. If you change your mind about deleting a particular slide, click the No button. The slide deletes and the other slides in the show renumber.

In this lesson, you learned how to choose a slide show master and apply a template to it so that you can begin to create your own slide show, and how to add and delete slides. In the next lesson, you will learn how to add text to your slides by using the WP Presentations Outliner.

Lesson 4

Using the Outliner to Add Text to a Slide

In this lesson, you will learn how to enter text into your slides by using the Outliner and how to create a bulleted list on a slide.

Opening the Outliner Window

After choosing a slide show master and a template, as explained in Lesson 3, you can use the Outliner to add text to your slides. The Outliner is one of two ways to add text to a slide. The second method, which involves using the Presentations Text Tool, is covered in the next lesson. Think of the Outliner as a feature that helps you organize the text for a slide in an outline format. An outline is an excellent way to organize your thoughts, so it's often useful to begin adding text with the Outliner. To open the Outline window, perform these steps:

1. Click on the Outliner button on the bottom of the Presentations window, or open the View menu and click on Slide Show and then Outliner. The Outliner window appears (see Figure 4.1).

2. If you haven't already done so, click on the Template pop-up list button located at the bottom of the screen and select the template you want to use for your slide.

Outliner window

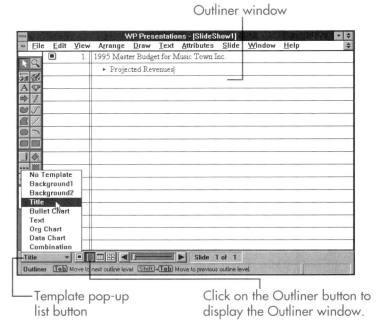

Template pop-up
list button

Click on the Outliner button to
display the Outliner window.

Figure 4.1   Opening the Outliner window.

Creating Text Slides Using the Outliner

With the Outliner window open and a template chosen, you
can begin adding titles, subtitles, main points, and more to
your slides. The Outliner is the easiest way to set up titles
and subtitles. Follow these steps:

1. On the first line of the Outliner window, type a title
   for the first slide, and press Enter. The insertion
   point moves to the next line.

2. Press Tab. A small arrow appears, and the insertion
   point moves to the right, a bit indented.

3. Type the subtitle (see Figure 4.2). To add another
   level (lower level) of text, press Enter and then
   press Tab. You can add different levels of text to a

slide using the Outliner. The title is the highest level, followed by subtitle, main points, and secondary points. You move down a level each time you press Tab.

4. Click on the Slide button at the bottom of the screen to bring the slide back into view.

> **Shortcut Keys**   To move to a previous outline level, press Shift+Tab.

Enter the title for the slide here, press return, and press Tab to move to the next line so you can enter the subtitle.

Enter subtitle here.

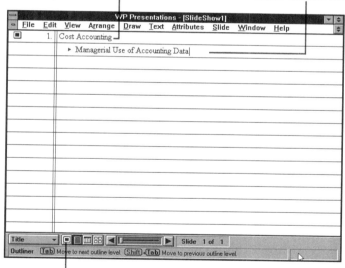

Click here (Slide button) to bring the slide back into view.

Figure 4.2   Entering titles and subtitles into the Outliner window.

Creating a Bulleted List Using the Outliner

A bulleted list is made with the Bullet chart template and lists your text with a symbol, such as a small, filled circle or triangle, in front of each item in the list. To create a bulleted list:

1. Click on the Outliner button at the bottom of the Presentations window, or open the View menu, click on Slide Show and then Outliner. The Outliner window appears.

2. Click on the Template pop-up list button and select Bullet Chart.

3. Type the title for the slide and press Enter. The insertion point will move to the next line.

4. Press Tab. A small arrow appears, and the insertion point moves to the right, a bit indented. This creates an indent from the previous line for inserting secondary points about the main bulleted topic.

5. Type the text for the first bullet.

6. Press Enter and type the text for the second bullet. Repeat this step until you have typed all the bulleted text for the slide.

7. Click on the Slide button at the bottom of the screen to bring the slide back into view as shown in Figure 4.3. If you want to create more bulleted slides, add more slides, and then follow steps 3–6.

Adding a Slide   If you want to learn how to add a slide, see Lesson 3.

Title

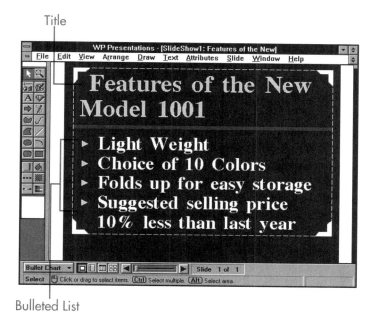

Bulleted List

Figure 4.3   Bullet slide.

Editing Text Using the Outliner

After creating a text slide or a bulleted list using the Outliner, you may need to do some editing. Editing in the Outliner is similar to editing with a word processing program. Simply move the insertion point by using the mouse and clicking at the point where you want to make changes. While in the Outliner, you have access to the Edit menu, which allows you to delete, cut and paste, and copy text.

To edit text in the Outliner, follow these steps:

1. Use your mouse to move the insertion point to where you want to begin editing. If you want to make changes in the middle of a word, click the insertion point where you want to make your changes. Press Backspace to delete a character to

the left of the insertion point. Drag the insertion point over an entire word or phrase that you want to copy or delete.

2. After positioning the insertion point, you can type your changes, and you can open the Edit menu and use the following commands:

Command	What It Does
Delete	Removes the highlighted text from the Outliner.
Cut	Removes the highlighted text from the Outliner and places it on the Microsoft Windows Clipboard so that you can paste it at some other place in the Outliner or in another Windows application.
Copy	Removes a copy of the highlighted text from the Outliner and places it on the Microsoft Windows Clipboard so that you can paste it at some other place in the Outliner or in another Windows application.
Paste	Places text (that you had previously copied or cut) from the Clipboard into the Outliner.

Copying Text to the Windows Clipboard

If you want to copy the deleted text to the Clipboard, use Edit Cut. When you use Edit Delete, the text is not placed on the Windows Clipboard. This means that you cannot use it in another application or in another Presentations text area.

Undo   If you edit the text in the Outliner and then decide that you want to revert back to the text as it was before your editing, you can use the Edit Undo command. Undo reverses your most recent change. To undo your last edit, open the Edit menu, and click on Undo.

In this lesson, you learned to use the Outliner to add text to slides, to create slides containing bulleted lists, and to edit your slides. In the next lesson, you will learn about another way to add text to your slides using the Text Tool.

Lesson

Adding and Editing Text Using the Text Tool

In this lesson, you will learn how to add text to a slide using the Text Tool. You will also learn how to edit, move, and delete text.

In Lesson 4, you learned how to add text to a slide by using the Outliner. In this lesson, you will learn how to add text directly to the slide using the Text Tool feature. The Text Tool is the small icon that looks like an uppercase A located in the tool palette (to the left of the slide window).

To add text to a slide, you begin by clicking on the Text Tool which allows you to add text in two ways. You can add a text line (a single line of text) or you can add a text area (a block of text), such as a paragraph. The advantage of adding text directly to the slide using the Text Tool is that WP Presentations treats the text as an object, which means you can size, move, and delete it with relative ease.

Object A line or block of text, a drawing, figure, or chart that you add to a slide. An object occupies a rectangular space or area on a slide. You can select objects by pointing at them and clicking. By selecting an object, you can move it, size it, or delete it.

Plain English

Adding a Text Line

A text line is a single line of text. To create the text line, you must first open or set up a text line box, into which you will type your text. To add a line of text, follow these steps:

1. Click on the Text Tool button on the tool palette, or open the Draw menu choose click on Text.

2. Click the slide window area near the left margin. A text line box appears across the screen.

3. Type the text you want entered on the slide (see Figure 5.1).

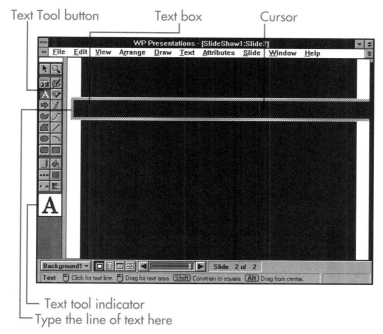

Figure 5.1   Creating a text box.

4. Press Enter, or click the right mouse button. WP Presentations adds the text to the slide. If you want to edit or move the text, see the sections that follow.

Tool Palette   An area to the left of the slide
window that contains the text, drawing, and
charting tool icons.

To change text fonts and other characteristics, such as
color, see Lesson 15.

Adding a Block of Text

Instead of adding just one line of text, you can add a block of
text, such as a paragraph or a list. Adding a block of text
works much like adding a text line. First, you must create an
area (called a *text area*) into which you can type your text.
To create a block of text, follow these steps:

1. Click on the Text Tool button on the tool palette, or
open the Draw menu and click on Text.

2. Move the mouse pointer (it looks like a cross) to
where you want to create a text area.

3. Click and hold the mouse button while you drag the
mouse pointer to form the text area (box). Release
the mouse button when you have formed a box that
is approximately the size you want. The cursor
appears as a vertical bar in the upper left corner of
the text box.

4. Type the text you want to appear in the text box.
As you type, the words wrap to the next line, and if
you want to start a new paragraph in the text box,
press Enter.

5. To close the text box, click once outside the box,
select another tool from the tool palette, or press
the right mouse button and highlight the Exit Text
Editor from the pop-up menu.

Editing Text

You can make changes to the text that you have added to a slide but you must first open the text line or area that holds the text. When you open the text area, you are in the Presentations Text Editor, which allows you to move the text insertion point to where you want to make changes and edit. You can add or delete characters, edit existing text, and close the text area. To edit text, follow these steps:

> **Insertion Point**   A blinking vertical line (sometimes called a cursor) that appears whenever WP Presentations allows you to enter text. You see the insertion point in the text lines, text areas, on the Outliner, and in dialog boxes.

1. Select the text you want to edit by clicking anywhere on it. To select text, you must first click on the Select tool icon in the tools palette (that's the one in the top left corner of the palette that looks like the mouse pointer). Once you have selected the text, little squares called *handles* appear around the text, forming a box or rectangle (see Figure 5.2).

2. Double-click within the selected text or place the pointer on the selected text, press the right mouse button, and choose Edit Text from the pop-up quick edit menu. A text area called the Text Editor opens.

3. Now you can select and modify any part of the text by moving the text insertion point (the vertical blinking line). You can use the mouse or the arrow keys on your keyboard to move the insertion point inside the text area.

4. Perform the editing. To learn how to delete selected characters or words, see the "Deleting Only Selected Text" section in this lesson. To change the text font, color, and other attributes, see Lesson 16, "Changing Text."

The Select tool icon must be selected before you
can use the mouse pointer to select objects.

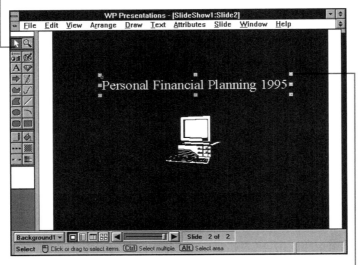

These little squares are called handles;
they appear when you select the text.

Figure 5.2   Selecting text.

5. To exit the Text Editor, click outside the text area,
or press the right mouse button and highlight Exit
Text Editor.

> **Spell Checking Your Text**   You also can
> use Presentations to check the spelling of your
> text. See Lesson 17 for more details.

Moving Text

Once you add text to a slide, its initial position on the slide
will probably not be where you want it. You can move text
easily because your lines of text are one object. This means

you can select the entire chunk of text to move it (drag it) around the slide in one piece. To reposition text, follow these steps:

1. Select the text you want to move by clicking on it. You know when you have properly selected the text (or any object) because little squares called handles appear around the text forming a box or rectangle.

2. Move the mouse pointer onto the selected text; click and drag the text to the new location.

3. Release the mouse button. The text moves to the next location.

Bad Move   If you don't like the new location, you can send the text back to its premove location by using Edit Undo or by pressing Ctrl+Z.

Deleting the Entire Text Object

You can delete some or all of the text. Since the text is an object, you can select it as one item and delete it from the slide. Also, as you will see in the next section of this lesson, you can delete only selected text within a text line or area. When you delete text, you lose it. Therefore, keep in mind that once you delete it, text cannot be used again.

Delete Wrong Text?   Presentations does not place deleted text on the Windows Clipboard (temporary storage area that helps you transfer information between documents and applications) as is the case when you cut or copy text. To retrieve it, select Edit Undo. You must do this immediately after you have deleted the text, before you press any other keys.

To delete a line of text or an entire text area in one quick command, follow these steps:

1. Select the text by clicking on it. Handles appear around the text.

2. Open the Edit menu and select Delete. WP Presentations deletes the text from the slide.

Shortcut Keys   After selecting the text, you can delete it by pressing the Del key.

If you want to delete several text areas at the same time, perform the following steps:

1. Select a group of text items by clicking on the Select Tool icon in the tools palette.

2. Place the mouse at the upper left corner of all the text areas you want to delete, hold down the mouse button, and drag the mouse across all text items that you want to delete.

3. When all the text areas you want to delete are within the outlined area created by dragging the mouse, release the mouse button. Handles appear around the selected text objects.

4. Press the Del key, or use Edit Delete to delete them all.

Deleting Only Selected Text

You may need to delete selected text within the text object, instead of deleting an entire text object. To do this type of selective editing, you must open the text area that contains the text you want to delete. With the text area opened, you can highlight the text with the insertion point and delete it. To delete only selected text, follow these steps:

1. Open the text line or box by double-clicking on the text. The text area opens.

2. Select the text by dragging the insertion point (vertical line) across the text. The text becomes highlighted.

3. Open the Edit menu, and select Delete, or press the Delete key. Presentations deletes the text from the slide.

> **Copying Text to the Windows Clipboard**
> If you delete text by using Edit Delete, Presentations doesn't place the text on the Windows Clipboard. This means that you cannot use it in another application or in another Presentations text area. If you want to move the deleted text to the Clipboard, use Edit Cut.

In this lesson, you learned how to add text to a slide and how to move, edit, and delete that text. In the next lesson, you can learn how to add art work and other graphics to a slide to enhance your messages.

Lesson

Adding Figures to Your Presentation

In this lesson, you will learn how to add figures from the Presentations Figure Gallery and other sources to your WP Presentations slide shows. You will also learn how to locate your figure files.

Adding Figures from the Figure Gallery

When you are designing a presentation or slide show, you may want to add pictures to the words on the slide to emphasize and break up the text, add humor, or graphically show what charts, bullet lists, and paragraphs cannot clearly explain. WP Presentations comes with 22 sets of figures, called *categories*, in a *figure gallery* for just this purpose. Each category contains several figures that depict different aspects of that particular category. For example, there is a Business category in the Figure Gallery. Within the Business category are 61 figures that relate to business, such as business and manufacturing equipment, people in business meetings, business supplies, charts and graphs, and others. If you are creating a slide that presents data on a rising stock market, you can add a figure of a bull to the slide.

Figures The WP Presentations term for charts, drawings, or other images you can insert into a slide show. In many other applications, figures are called *clip art*.

To add a figure to a slide that exists in the Figure Gallery, follow these steps:

1. You must be in the Presentations Document window (Lesson 1) or have opened a previously saved slide show (Lesson 7).

2. Click on the Figure tool in the tool palette, or open the Draw menu and click on Figure. The mouse pointer turns into a hand holding a square.

3. Place the pointer on the slide where you want to insert the figure and drag the mouse to create an area for the figure. If you want the figure to take up the whole slide, just click once to create a full-page figure. The Figure Gallery dialog box appears (see Figure 6.1).

4. To see all the categories available in the gallery, click on the up and down arrows of the scroll bar. When you find the category you want, click on the sketch of that category.

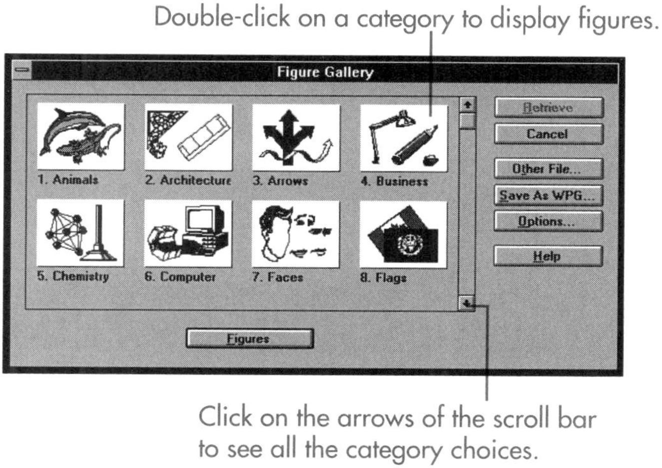

Double-click on a category to display figures.

Click on the arrows of the scroll bar to see all the category choices.

Figure 6.1   Adding a figure to a slide.

5. Click on the Figures button to view miniature versions of the figures in the selected category. The figures appear, eight at a time. Use the arrows on the scroll bar to see all the figures contained in the category.

6. Click on the figure you want, and click on the Retrieve button. WP Presentations adds the figure to the slide.

Moving and Resizing Clip Art

After you insert clip art into your slide show, you will probably need to move it or resize it. To move or resize a graphic, follow these steps:

1. Click on the Select tool.

2. Click the clip art. Handles (small boxes) will surround the selected graphic.

3. To move the graphic, move the mouse pointer so it is on some part of the graphic but not on the handles. Click and hold the right mouse button and drag the graphic to the new location. When you have it where you want it, release the mouse button.

4. To resize the graphic, place the mouse pointer on any handle; press and drag.

> You can also resize the graphic by placing the mouse pointer on any handle and pressing the right mouse button. The Stretch dialog box appears. Enter in the Multiplier text box a number for how much larger or smaller you want the object.

Adding Figures That Are Not in the Gallery

You don't have to restrict your artwork to those figures found in the Figure Gallery. You can add scanned images, clip art, and drawings created in other graphics programs to your slides. *Clip art* is a collection of professionally drawn figures you can insert into your word processing, spreadsheet, slide show, or other applications.

If you have some artistic flair, you can create your own artwork with any drawing program, or use the drawing tools in WP Presentations to create a graphic file you can add to slides. Of course, to work with other graphics, you must save the files on a floppy disk or in a directory on your hard drive. You must save graphics created in other applications to the right format before Presentations will recognize and import them. To add figures that are not in the gallery, follow these steps:

1. You must be in the Presentations Document window (Lesson 1) or have opened a previously saved slide show (Lesson 7).

2. Click on the Figure tool in the tool palette, or open the Draw menu and click on Figure. The mouse pointer turns into a hand holding a square.

3. Place the pointer on the slide where you want to insert the figure and drag the mouse to create an area for the figure. If you want the figure to take up the whole slide, click once to create a full-page figure. The Figure Gallery dialog box appears.

4. Click on the Other File button. The Retrieve Figure dialog box appears. Enter the path and filename of the figure in the Filename text box, and click the Retrieve button. The figure appears in your slide.

For more information on the graphics file formats that you can import into WP Presentations, consult the Reference Guide.

5. You can also find the figure's drive and directory by clicking on the directories in the Directories list box until the correct path appears under the Filename text box. Your file will appear in the Files list box. Click on the file name in the Files list box, and the file you want to retrieve will appear in the Filename text box. Then click on the Retrieve button.

Locating Figure Files

When you are inserting graphics that are not part of the Figure Gallery into your slide show, you always have to tell WP Presentations which directory to retrieve the graphics from. You can retrieve figures and slide shows by the method described in the previous section. However, to save you some time, WP Presentations has a default directory for figures and clip art called c:\prwin\clipart. You can copy your files to this directory, and WP Presentations will always look there first for your files. You can change this default directory path if this name is not meaningful to you or if you want to reorganize your directories. You must first create these directories on your hard drive before you can set them from within WP Presentations. To specify the directory for your own figure files, follow these steps:

1. Open the File menu and click on Preferences. The Preferences dialog box appears.

2. Double click on the Location of Files icon. The Location of Files dialog box appears (see Figure 6.2).

3. Type the pathname for your figure and clip art files in the Figures/Clip Art text box.

Enter the name of the directory where you
want to locate your figures and clip art.

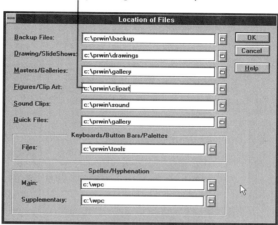

Figure 6.2 Locating figure files.

4. Click on the OK button; then click on the Close
button.

In this lesson, you learned how to add graphic images to
your slide shows from the WP Presentations Figure Gallery
and other sources. You also learned how to set default
directories to conveniently locate your graphics files. In the
next lesson, you will learn how to save, close, and open your
slide show.

Lesson

Saving, Closing, and Opening Slide Shows

In this lesson you will learn how to save a new slide show to a file, how to close a slide show file when you finish working with it, and how to open a previously saved slide show.

Saving a Slide Show

After you create a series of slides, you need to save them in a slide show file. To save your new slide show for the first time, you must use the File Save As or Save command from the menu bar. The File Save As command allows you to assign a unique name to the new file and lets you save the new file to the directory of your choice. You also have the option to save your new file to a floppy disk. You also need to use the File Save As command when you want to save an existing slide show under a new filename or you want to save it to a new directory.

A filename consists of up to eight characters. You can use both letters and numbers in a filename, along with these characters:

~ ! @ # $ % ^ & ( ) - {} _

When you save your slide show file, WP Presentations automatically adds the **.SHW** extension to the end of the filename that you specify. This extension helps you distinguish between your slide show files and other files you may have in your directory or on your floppy disk.

To save your new slide show, follow these steps:

1. Open the File menu, and click on Save As, or press F3. As shown in Figure 7.1, the Save As dialog box appears.

Type the filename here.

Select the directory you want to save the file to by clicking here to display a list of directories.

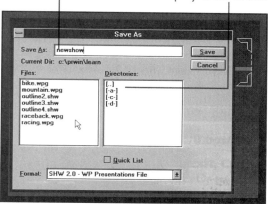

Figure 7.1 Saving a new slide show.

2. Type a unique filename for the new file in the Save As filename text box. If you are saving the file to the current directory, you need only to type the filename. The current directory is shown in the Save As dialog box, just below the filename text box. It is the default directory to which WP Presentations saves files and from which it opens files. If you want to save the file to another directory, double-click the [..] in the first line of the Directories box to display a list of directories. Then select the directory by double-clicking on it. The directory will be added to the pathname in the Save As text box.

Pathname   The address of a file. A full pathname includes the drive, the root directory, any subdirectory names, and the filename. For example, c:\prwin\newshow.shw.

3. Click on the Save button. WP Presentations saves your file and you return to your slide show.

Default Settings   Default settings are options, features, and values that WP Presentations automatically provides. You can change these settings, which affect future slide shows that you create, if you specify an alternative.

If you are working on a slide show that already exists on disk and you want to replace it with your new version, choose File Save from the menu bar, press Shift+F3, or click on the Save button on the Button Bar.

Closing a Slide Show

Closing a slide show is different from exiting WP Presentations. Exiting WP Presentations takes you completely out of the program and leaves you at the WP Presentations group icon in Windows. When you close a slide show file, however, you simply exit from that file, but you remain within the WP Presentations application. You can continue working in WP Presentations by creating a new slide show or opening an existing slide show. You can close out of a slide show at any time. To close a slide show without exiting from WP Presentations, follow these steps:

1. Open the File menu, and click on Close.

2. If you have changed the slide show since the last time you saved it, click on Yes to save the changes and close the document. If you don't want to save the changes that you made to the slide show, choose No to close the file without saving the changes.

Shortcut Keys   To quickly close a file, click on the Close button on the Button Bar or press Ctrl+F4.

Opening a Slide Show

You may decide to make changes to a slide show file that you have previously saved and closed. To work with an existing slide show, you must first open its file by following these steps:

1. Open the File menu and click on Open, or click on the Open button on the Button Bar or press F4. The Open File dialog box appears, as shown in Figure 7.2.

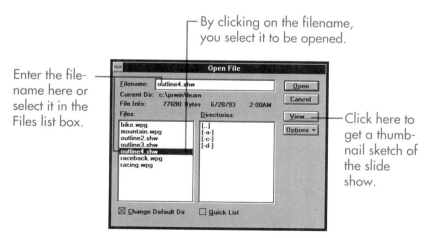

Figure 7.2   Opening a file.

2. Type the name of the file you want to open in the Filename text box, or double-click on the filename inside the Files list box.

3. To see a thumbnail sketch of the slide show before you open the file, click on the View button (see Figure 7.3).

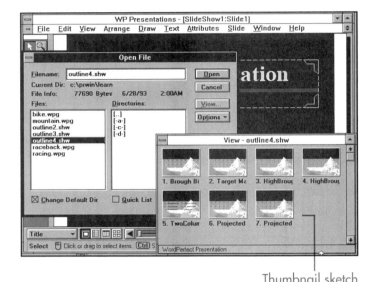

Thumbnail sketch
of a slide show

Figure 7.3 A thumbnail sketch of a slide show.

Opening More Than One File   To open more than one file at a time, hold down the Ctrl key while you click on the files.

4. Click on the Open button. The first slide appears.

In this chapter, you learned how to save, close, and open slide show files. In the next lesson, you learn how to play a slide show.

Lesson

8

Learning to Play a Slide Show

In this lesson, you will learn how to play a slide show, use a highlighter, and make a run-time version of your slide show so you can play it on other PCs.

Playing a Slide Show

You have created a slide show file that contains all the important information you want to say at your meeting. Now you want to see the effects of your handiwork by playing back the slides. Before you can play a slide show, you must open the slide show file using the steps outlined in Lesson 7. Then you must decide if you want to advance each slide manually or automatically. Advancing each slide manually means you will control when to play the next slide by clicking the mouse buttons. To advance slides automatically means you will set a specific amount of time between the playing of each slide, and the computer will advance them for you. With the slide show file open, follow these steps to play the slide show:

1. Open the Slide menu, and click on Transition. The Slide Transition dialog box appears (see Figure 8.1).

2. Click on Manual to manually advance one slide at a time. Click on Timed, and WP Presentations advances the slides using an automatic delay. If you choose Timed, enter the number of seconds you want the slide show to pause before advancing to the next slide in the Seconds to Delay box.

Click here to control when to
advance to the next slide.

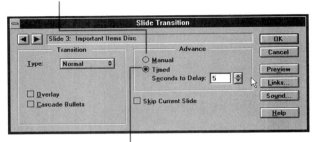

Click here and WP Presentations automatically
advances to the next slide at timed intervals.

Figure 8.1   Setting how the slides will advance.

3. When you have made your choices, click on the OK
button to save them.

4. Open the Slide menu, and click on Play Slide Show.
The Play Slide Show dialog box appears.

5. Click on Play to run your slide show. To leave the
slide show, press Esc.

If you set the Advance to manual, you control the
advancement of slides. You manually advance slides by
clicking the right mouse button to go forward one slide and
clicking the left mouse button to go back one slide.

If you set the Advance to Timed, WP Presentations
automatically displays each slide in sequential order at the
time intervals you specified.

Using the Highlighter

WP Presentations has a feature called the Highlighter. As the
name implies, this feature enables you to use your mouse to
highlight items on your slides while playing a slide show. To
use the highlighter, follow these steps:

1. Play a slide show as outlined in the previous section.

2. When you want to highlight an item, move the mouse to the area of the slide that you want to highlight, hold down the left mouse button, and drag the mouse to underline, circle, draw arrows, and so on—whatever you want to do to emphasize an item (see Figure 8.2). The highlight appears wherever you drag, but it's temporary; it does not permanently mark up your slides.

Use the highlighter to circle text.

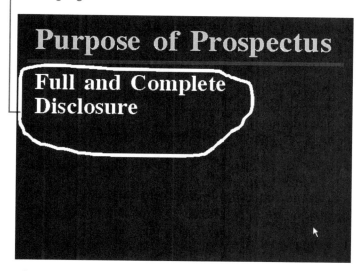

Figure 8.2   Highlighting important points.

Changing the Color and Line Width of the Highlighter

You can change both the color and the width of the line you draw with the highlighter by following these steps:

1. Open the Slide menu and click on Play Slide Show. The Play Slide Show dialog box appears.

2. Under Highlighter Color, click on the color palette, which is represented by a colored square. The color palette appears.

3. Select a highlighter color from the color palette by clicking on one of the color squares. The color you have chosen appears.

4. Specify a Line Width by entering a number in the Highlighter Width box, or click on the Line Width icon to select a line width. Enter a number to select the line width.

5. Click on the Play button to start the slide show.

Creating Quick Files to Speed Up the Show

To create snappier slide shows that take less time to appear on the screen, you can use the WP Presentations Quick File feature. Quick File saves an entire slide show as bit-map images. Your computer can display a bit-map image much faster than it can redraw your screen each time you play a new slide. A Quick File essentially has no time delay. However, even though a Quick File speeds up the slide show, it uses more memory. For example, the slide show Outline4.shw in the WP Presentations learn subdirectory is 77,680 bytes. The same file converted to a Quick File will need over 330,000 bytes of memory—over 320% more space.

To create a Quick File follow these steps:

1. Open the slide show you want to play as described in Lesson 7.

2. Open the Slide menu, and click on Play Slide Show. The Play Slide Show dialog box appears.

3. Click on the Create Quick File button, as shown in Figure 8.3. The slide show plays as WP Presentations creates the Quick File (bit-map images).

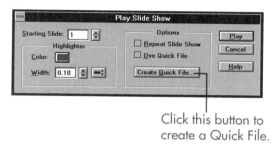

Click this button to
create a Quick File.

Figure 8.3   Creating a Quick File.

4. Click the Play button. The Quick File slide show will play.

What If I Change the Slides?   If you create a Quick File for one of your slide shows and then you decide to change the slides, you must re-create the Quick File after you have changed your slide show file. Quick Files are bit maps, or pictures of slides. If you change a slide, you must retake the pictures (Quick Files) to reflect the new show.

Making a Run-Time Version of a Slide Show

You can also create slide shows that will run on other computers—even those PCs that do not have WP Presentations installed. To create this stand-alone slide show software, you need to create a *run-time version* of your slide show. When you save a run-time version of your slide show, WP Presentations copies the necessary program files to a

disk so you can run them on other computers. WP Presentations stores a run-time slide show in two files: one with a
.SHW extension and one with a .PQW extension. For example, if you create a slide show named MUTUALS and it is a
run-time version, then WP Presentations creates two files:
MUTUALS.SHW and MUTUALS.PRQ. You need both files to
run the program on a PC that does not have WP Presentations installed. Keep that in mind if you decide to rename the
run-time files. You will have to give them both the same
filename, with the .SHW and .PQW extensions.

To create a run-time version of one of your slide shows,
follow these steps:

1. Create or open a slide show. If you created a new
slide show, save it, and then move on to step 2.

2. Open the Slide menu, and click on Make Run-time.
The Make Run-time dialog box appears (see Figure
8.4).

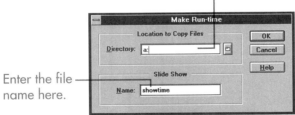

Enter the location (drive and directory) of
where you want to copy the run-time files to.

Enter the file
name here.

Figure 8.4   Creating a run-time version of a slide show.

3. Enter the name you want to give to the slide show
file and specify the location (disk drive, directory)
for the file.

4. Click on the OK button to create the run-time file of
your slide show.

Viewing a Run-time Slide Show

When you want to view the run-time slide show on another PC, you must use the Windows Program Manager to get the show up and running. You can run the show from the disk or copy it to the hard drive. To view the run-time version on another PC, follow these steps:

1. Open the File menu from the Windows Program Manger.

2. Click on Run. The Run dialog box appears.

3. In the Command line text box enter the filename of the run-time slide show. Be sure to specify drive\directory\filename. For example, if you named your slide show, SHOW1, and it is on the disk in drive A, type **A:\SHOW1**.

4. Click on the OK button and the show will begin. You can stop the slide show at any time by pressing Esc. If you set the run-time slide show for a time delay advance of slides, that will also be the case in the run-time version. If you set the advance to manual, you must press the right mouse button to advance forward and the left mouse button to go backward.

Run-Time on Another PC Your run-time slide show can be run on a 386 or higher PC. If you create it on a 486 and run it on a 386, you will notice that it does run a little slower.

In this lesson, you learned to play a slide show, use the highlighter to give emphasis, create a run-time version (stand-alone) of a slide show, and how to run a run-time slide show. The next lesson shows you how to print your slide show so that you can use it for handouts or notes.

Lesson

Printing Presentations

In this lesson, you will learn how to set up your slide show for printing, how to print it, and how to create and print speaker notes that you can refer to as you play the slide show.

Setting Up Your Presentation for Printing

If you have printed a word processing document or a spreadsheet, then you know that you may need to change the layout of your pages before you print. With WP Presentations, you may need to make some basic changes to your layout before printing. The two common changes are 1) to change the margins and the page layout, and 2) to select a landscape or portrait orientation. To set up the page layout, follow these steps:

1. Open or create a slide show.

2. Open the File menu, and click on Page Layout. Or if you want to change the page layout for all slides in your slide show, open the File menu, click on Preferences, and double-click on the Page Layout icon. The Page Layout dialog box appears (see Figure 9.1).

3. If you want to change the size of the margins, enter new settings in the margin boxes, or click the arrows to increase or decrease the margin sizes.

Click here to change page size.   Change margins.

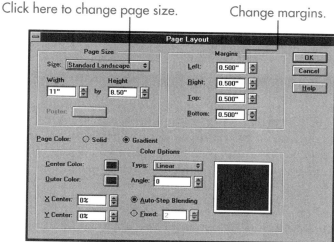

Figure 9.1   Changing the page layout.

4. If you want to change the size of the page, click on the Size pop-up list button, and choose one of the following:

Table 9.1   Page Size Options

Size	Width	Height
Standard	8.5-inch	11-inch
Standard Landscape	11-inch	8.5-inch
Legal	8.5-inch	14-inch
Legal Landscape	14-inch	8.5-inch
Envelope	9.5-inch	4-inch
35MM	11-inch	7.33-inch

continues

Table 9.1   Continued

Size	Width	Height
US Government	8-inch	11-inch
A4	8.27-inch	11.69-inch
A4 Landscape	11.69-inch	8.27-inch
Other	You set the width and height	

5. Click on the OK button. If you make your changes using File Preferences, click on Yes to update the entire slide show, and click on the Close button to exit the Preferences box.

> **Portrait vs. Landscape**   A page in which the long edge of the page runs vertically (8.5 × 11-inch) is portrait as opposed to landscape which is a page with the long edge running horizontally (11 × 8.5-inch).

Selecting a Printer

If you have only one printer and you use it for your other Windows applications, such as word processing or spread-sheets, it will already be set up as your default printer for WP Presentations. However, if you use more than one printer, you have to tell WP Presentations which one you want to use. For example, if Windows is currently set up to use your laser printer but you now want to print your slides using your color deskjet printer, then you will have to follow these steps to change the printer:

1. Open the File menu and click on Print Setup. The Print Setup dialog box appears (see Figure 9.2).

2. In the Available Printers list box, click on the printer that you want to use.

Default printer is the one currently used
by WP Presentations to print slides.

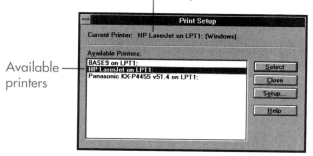

Available —
printers

Figure 9.2   Selecting a different printer.

3. Click on the Select button. The Print Setup dialog
box closes, and you can now print to the selected
printer.

Printing Your Slide Show

Once you create a slide show, selected a page layout, and if
necessary, selected a printer, you can print the slide show.
When you print a slide show, one slide prints per page. This
creates a professional package you can use for audience
handouts. To print the slide show, perform the following
steps:

1. Create or open the slide show you want to print.

2. Open the File menu, and click on Print. The Print
dialog box appears (see Figure 9.3).

3. Click on the Print pop-up list box, and click on
Slides.

4. If you want to look at the slides to see how they will
appear on the printed page before you actually print
them, click on the View button. Press Esc to return
to the Print dialog box.

Click here to select Slides from a pop-up list.

Select this box if you want to print all the slides in the show.

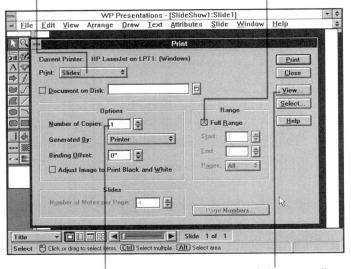

Enter the number of copies you want to print here.

To view a slide as it will appear printed, click here.

Figure 9.3 Printing a slide show.

5. If you want to print the entire slide show, click on the Full Range check box. If you only want to print part of the slide show, enter the number of the first and last slide you want to print in the Start and End boxes or use the arrows for those boxes to select a start and end number.

6. If you want to print more than one copy of the slide show, enter the number of copies you want to print in the Number of Copies box, or click the up and down arrows to select the number of copies to print.

Printing Part of a Slide Show To specify the start and end slides, first deselect (clear) the Full Range check box.

7. Click on the Print button.

Creating and Printing Speaker Notes

To help you present a successful slide show, you can generate speaker notes, which prompt you about the key points of each slide as it appears. The speaker notes are pages of thumbnail sketches of each slide with notes under each slide that only you will see.

To create and print speaker notes follow these steps:

1. Open the Slide menu, and click on Speaker Notes. The Speaker Notes dialog box appears (see Figure 9.4).

Click the arrow buttons to select the slide you want to add speaker notes to.

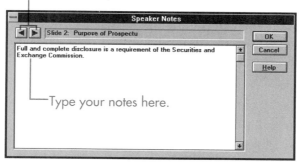

Figure 9.4 Creating speaker notes.

2. Specify the number of the slide you want to add speaker notes to by using the arrow buttons.

3. Type a note for the slide in the note box.

4. Repeat steps 2 and 3 until you have typed all the notes you want.

5. Click on the OK button.

6. Open the File menu, and click on Print. The Print dialog box appears.

7. Click on the Print pop-up list, and select Speaker Notes.

8. Click on the Print button.

> **Handouts**   If you want to give the audience a handout that shows all the slides in your slide show in just a few pages, select Handouts in step 7 above. Each page will contain from 1 to 16 printed slides, rather than one slide to a page, when you print the slide show. You can set this number in the Number of Slides per Page box. Six is the default number of slides that WP Presentations will display.

In this chapter, you learned how to set up your slide show so that you can print it and how to create speaker notes that can enhance your delivery of the slide show. In the next lesson, you will learn how to create organization charts with WP Presentations.

Lesson

10

Creating an Organization Chart

In this lesson, you will learn how to create organization charts using the Org Chart template and the Chart tool, and how to add staff positions to your organization chart.

Adding an Organization Chart to a Slide

Quite often when you present business or marketing concepts to potential customers or investors, they want to know how your company is organized, who the decision makers are, and what staff is available to support the organization. WP Presentations has two features that make it very easy to create an organizational chart. The first feature is an organization chart template (Slide show templates were discussed in Lesson 4), and the second is the Chart tool, found in the tool palette.

When creating organization charts, keep a few simple rules in mind:

- For clarity and consistency, use either position names, such as Vice President or Manager, or people names in all boxes throughout the organization chart.

- Avoid showing too much information. This can be distracting and make the chart confusing.

- For most charts, a top-to-bottom orientation is best. This is the traditional layout and the easiest to read.

- Think about the level of authority of each position: Is the person a manager, directly responsible for the product or service being offered by the company (a *line position*), or is the person in a support or administrative role, such as a bookkeeper or assistant (a *staff position*)? WP Presentations makes a distinction between line and staff positions. A separate section in this lesson discusses staff positions.

Creating and Editing an Organization Chart Using the Template

A *template* is a predesigned slide that you can quickly modify to meet your needs. There is a Org Chart template that you can modify to reflect your own organization. This template uses a top-to-bottom layout, which is the traditional organization chart design. To create an organization chart using the template, follow these steps:

> Top-to-bottom is the traditional layout of an organization chart with the subordinate positions vertically below the supervisor.

1. Add a new slide by opening the Slide menu and clicking on Add Slide. Select Org chart from the Template pop-up list, and click on the OK button.

2. If you want to create an organization chart in an existing slide, click on the pop-up template list button located at the bottom left of the Presentations window (see Figure 10.1), and select Org Chart. An organizational chart template appears on your slide.

The Select tool

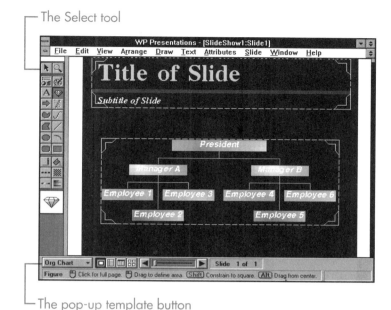

The pop-up template button

Figure 10.1   Selecting the Organization Chart template.

3. Click on the Select tool in the tool palette (see Figure 10.1), and double-click in the organization chart to open the Chart Editor. To make changes to the Org Chart template (or any template), you must be in the Chart Editor. As shown in Figure 10.2, the Outliner opens and appears above the organization chart in a split screen. The status bar at the bottom of the screen will also indicate that you are in the Chart Editor.

4. You can edit the sample data by positioning the insertion point in the Outliner on the org chart position you want to change and typing your changes. You can also clear all the sample data from the Outliner by opening the File menu, clicking on Clear, and choosing Yes.

Chart tool palette Outliner

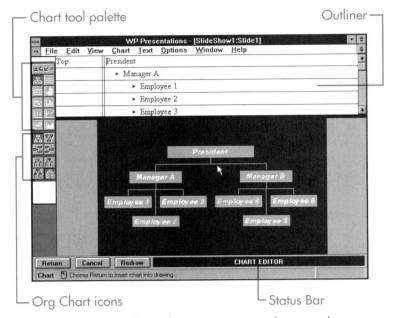

Org Chart icons Status Bar

Figure 10.2 Editing the Organization Chart template.

Shortcut Keys To quickly clear the sample organization chart text in the Outliner, press Ctrl+Shift+F4.

5. On the first line of the outline, type the name and/or title of the person you want at the top of the chart—for example, **Mary Smith, President**.

6. Press Enter to add a subordinate position, and type the name and or title of that person. Use the following keystrokes to create the remainder of the organization chart:

Keystrokes	Action
Enter	To add another position at the same level.
Enter; then Tab	To add a subordinate position.
Enter; then Shift+Tab	To add a superior position.

7. You can also use the WP Presentations Edit menu to help you create and change the positions and titles in your organization chart. While you are in the Chart Editor, the Edit menu contains these commands:

Command	Shortcut Keys
Delete	Del
Cut	Ctrl+X
Copy	Ctrl+C
Paste	Ctrl+V

8. After making your changes, click on the Redraw button at the bottom of the screen to update the organization chart.

9. Click on the Return button to exit the Chart Editor. Your organization chart appears.

Creating an Organization Chart Using the Chart tool

You can also create an organization chart using the Chart Editor and its palette of chart tools. To create an organization chart using the Chart editor, follow these steps:

1. Click on the Chart tool in the tool palette, as shown in Figure 10.3, or open the Draw menu, and select Chart.

Chart tool —

Figure 10.3 The Chart tool.

2. Click on the drawing window to create a chart that will fill the window, or position the mouse pointer in the place where you want the org chart to be located, and drag to define your own chart area. The Create Chart dialog box appears, as shown in Figure 10.4.

Click here to create an Organization chart.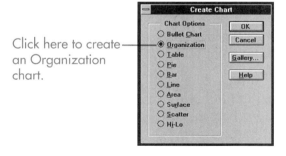

Figure 10.4 The Create Chart dialog box.

3. Click on the Organization option button and click on the OK button. The Chart Editor appears,

showing a split screen of the Text Chart Outliner and a sample organization chart. You will also see that a new palette of tools called the Chart tool palette has replaced the main tool palette on the left side of the screen.

4. Type your organization data in the Text Chart Outliner as described in the previous section. To completely clear the sample data, open the File menu, select Clear, and click on the Yes button to clear the text from the outline.

5. Click on the Chart Gallery tool in the Chart tool palette (see Figure 10.5). A gallery (thumbnail sketches) of 16 different organization chart types appear. Use the up and down arrows on the scroll bar to see all the org chart choices.

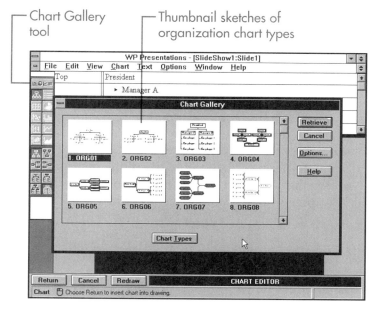

Figure 10.5 The Chart Gallery tool displays 16 organization chart types.

6. Click on the organization chart type that you want to use, and click on the Retrieve button. The new organization chart type appears.

Specifying Staff Positions on a Chart

Many organization charts show superior-to-subordinate relationships. However, not all positions in an organization flow in a top-down manner. There are *staff positions*: positions that carry no real authority in the organization hierarchy. A staff-level position may be an administrative assistant, secretary, or other personnel who are not part of the hierarchy. For example, the president's secretary is a staff position you can display on the organization chart near the president's position, but the secretary does not have authority over the vice president, whose position appears just below the secretary. WP Presentations displays staff positions away from the other positions using a dotted line to show that the position is not part of the hierarchy of authority. To add a staff position, follow these steps:

1. Open the Chart Editor by clicking on the Select tool in the tool palette and then double-clicking on the org chart.

2. In the Outliner, type the new entry that represents the staff position under the level of the management position to which it applies (that is, the manager to which the person in this staff position will report). You can also make an existing position a staff position.

3. Place the insertion point on the staff position and click.

4. Open the Options menu and click on Staff. The word staff appears in the first column of the Outliner.

5. Click on the Redraw button to update the organization chart. Figure 10.6 shows an organization chart
with a staff position.

Staff position

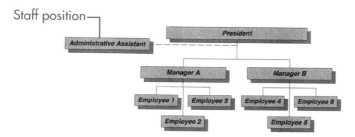

Figure 10.6 Adding staff positions to an organization chart.

Staff Position   If you want to change a staff
position back to a regular position in the hierarchy, place the insertion point on the Outliner at
the beginning of the staff position and choose Staff
from the Options menu.

In this lesson, you learned how to create and edit
organization charts using the Org Chart template and the
Chart tool. You also learned how to add staff positions to the
organization chart. In the next lesson, you will learn how to
customize your organization charts to meet your needs.

Lesson

Customizing Your Organization Chart

In this lesson, you will learn how to change the layout, border styles and shapes of the boxes, and line style of the connectors in your organization chart.

Changing the Layout of the Organization Chart

If the traditional top-to-bottom, pyramid-type organization chart does not suit your organizational approach, you can change the layout, or the *orientation*, of your chart. Four chart layouts are available through the Chart tool palette, which appears when you are in the Chart Editor. Although the top-to-bottom layout is traditional for showing the chain of command, and the default layout in WP Presentations, you can specify a bottom-to-top, left-to-right, or right-to-left chart layout by following these steps:

1. Click on the Select tool in the tool palette.

2. Double-click in the organization chart. The Chart Editor opens and the organization chart icons appear on the tool palette.

3. Click on the organization chart icon that depicts the chart orientation you want (see Figure 11.1). The layout of your chart changes.

4. Click on Return to exit the Chart Editor. Your Organization chart appears with its new orientation.

Top to bottom ⌐ ┌Bottom to top
Left to right ⌐ └Right to left

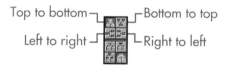

Figure 11.1 Organization Chart icons: changing the layout of the organization chart.

Changing the Look of the Boxes

You can do many things to change the look of the boxes in your organization chart. You can change the box shape to a rectangle or octagon, or you can decide to use no boxes at all. You can also choose from one of seven border styles, and you have the option of changing the color of boxes and borders. Colors, shapes, and line styles are all called *attributes*. To change the attributes of the boxes in your organization chart, follow these steps:

1. Click on the Select tool in the tool palette, and double-click on the organization chart. The Outliner and chart appear in a split screen.

2. Open the Options menu, and click on Box Attributes. The Box Attributes dialog box appears (see Figure 11.2).

3. If you want to change the shape of the boxes, or remove all boxes from the chart, click and hold the mouse button down to display the Box Style pop-up list. Highlight Rectangle, Rounded Rectangle, Octagon, or None (to remove all boxes) and release the mouse button.

4. If you want to change the color of the boxes, click and hold the mouse button to display the Fill Color Palette button and select your color choice.

Click here to change the color inside the boxes.

Click here to change the shape of the boxes.

Click here to change the color of the box borders.

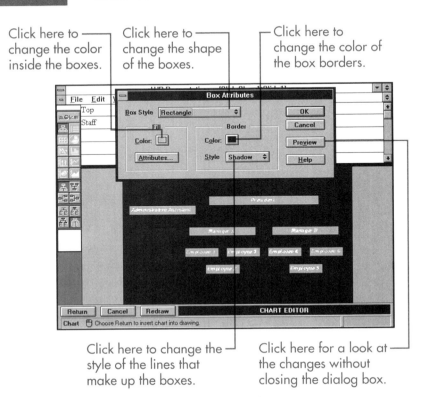

Click here to change the style of the lines that make up the boxes.

Click here for a look at the changes without closing the dialog box.

Figure 11.2   Changing box attributes.

5. If you want to change the color of the borders that surround the boxes, click on the Border Color palette to display the color palette. Click on your color choice.

6. If you want to change the style of the border around the boxes, click and hold the mouse button to display the Border Style pop-up list. Select one of the following styles from the list: Single, Double, Dotted, Dashed, Thick, Shadow, Beveled, or None.

7. When you have made all your attribute changes, click on the OK button. Your organization chart appears with the new attributes.

Changing the Style of the Connectors

The lines that connect different positions (levels) in the organization chart are called *connectors*. You can change the style and the color of connectors by following these steps:

1. Open the Chart Editor by clicking on the Select tool in the tool palette and double-clicking on the chart. The Outliner and chart appear in a split screen.

2. Open the Options menu and click on Connectors. The Connectors dialog box appears (see Figure 11.3). If it is not already selected, click on the Display Connectors check box to display chart connectors.

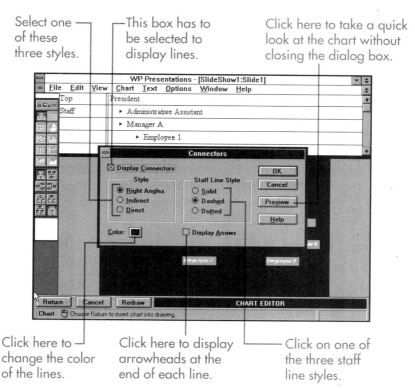

Figure 11.3 Changing organization chart connectors.

3. If you want to change the way lines connect the different levels of the org chart, click on one of the three options in the Style box: Right Angles, Indirect, Direct.

Right angle connectors are lines that are drawn as 90 degree angles. Indirect connectors are 45 degree angles; direct connectors are connecting lines that go straight from one box to another without an angle.

4. If you want to change the style of the lines connecting the staff positions, click on one of the three options in the Staff Line Style box: Solid, Dashed, Dotted.

5. If you want to change the color of all the connectors, click and hold the mouse button on the Color Palette button to display the color palette, and select your choice.

6. Sometimes arrowheads help show the flow of the organization chart. If you want the connector lines to have arrowheads, click on the Display Arrows check box.

7. To see the changes to the connectors without leaving the dialog box, click on the Preview button.

8. When you have made your changes to the connectors, click on the OK button.

9. Click on the Redraw button to redisplay the changed connectors, and click on the Return button to exit the Chart Editor.

In this lesson, you learned how to change the layout, border styles and shapes of the boxes, and line style of the connectors in your organization chart. In the next lesson, you will learn how to create data charts.

Lesson

12

Creating Data Charts

In this lesson, you will learn the basics of creating data charts, editing data charts, and importing data from other applications, such as a spreadsheet program.

Creating a Chart

Data charts, such as bar, pie, and line charts, can transform raw data into a powerful message. It's true that a picture can be worth a thousand words. To create a chart, you work with a data chart worksheet that looks very much like a spreadsheet that you would find in Lotus 1-2-3, Excel, or Quattro Pro. You enter your data in the worksheet, and the chart depicts the data graphically. To create a chart, follow these steps:

1. Click on the Chart tool in the tool palette.

2. Click in the drawing window to create a chart that will fill the window. Or place the pointer in the drawing window where you want the chart to appear, and drag in the drawing window to create your own chart area. The Create Chart dialog box appears.

3. Click on the data chart type you want, and click on the OK button. A split screen showing a worksheet and a chart appears (see Figure 12.1). The worksheet shows sample data in the chart.

Worksheet

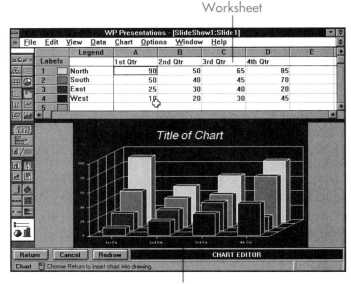

Chart depicts the data from the worksheet.

Figure 12.1   Entering the data you want to chart.

4. Enter data in the worksheet by clicking in the appropriate cell and typing your information (your data will replace the sample data). Or before entering your data, you can clear all the worksheet sample data by choosing Clear from the File menu.

Labels are text that you enter in the first row of the worksheet that describe the values, time period, or other descriptions of what you are charting. For example, if you are showing sales for each quarter in a bar chart, you could label the first bar as **1st Quarter**. The *legend* is a list of the colors, patterns, or symbols used for the bars, lines, or slices of pie in your chart. For example, the legend of a bar chart may show that the red bar is the sales for the northern region.

Shortcut Keys   Press Ctrl+Shift+F4 to clear the sample data from the data chart worksheet.

5. To change any of the colors used in the legend, double-click on the color you want to change. The colors are in the left-hand frame of the worksheet. The Series Option dialog box appears. Under Attributes, click on the color palette button to display the colors. Click on the new color; then click on the OK button. The color will change in both the legend (in the worksheet frame) and in the chart.

6. Click on the Redraw button to update the chart with your new data.

7. Click on the Return button to go back to the drawing window.

Editing the Worksheet

Use the worksheet to enter the data for your charts. If you want to change the data in your chart, you must edit the worksheet by following these steps:

1. Click on the Select tool in the tool palette.

2. Double-click in the chart you want to edit. This opens the Chart Editor.

3. Select a cell you want to edit in the worksheet by clicking on it. If you want to select a range of cells, click and drag the mouse over the range of cells. To select all cells in the worksheet, click on the upper-left corner of the worksheet, or choose Select All from the Edit menu.

> **Go To**   Press Ctrl+G to display the Go To dialog box, which allows you to type the address of a cell (such as A10) so that you can jump to that cell quickly.

4. Type the new data and press Enter, or click the right mouse button. You can also edit a cell by double-clicking in the cell to display the Edit Current Cell dialog box (see Figure 12.2). With that method of editing, you make your changes in the Cell text box, and click on the OK button.

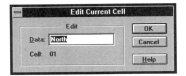

Figure 12.2   The Edit Current Cell dialog box.

5. The Edit menu in the Chart Editor contains these commands that you may also find useful when revising a worksheet:

Command	Action
Insert	Adds rows or columns.
Delete	Deletes rows or columns.
Clear	Erases the data in a cell, its format, or both.
Cut	Removes selected data from a Worksheet and places it in the Clipboard.
Copy	Inserts a copy of data from a Worksheet to the Clipboard.
Paste	Pastes the contents of the Clipboard into a Worksheet.
Paste Transposed	Switches the rows and columns of selected cells.
Select All	Selects all cells in a Worksheet.
Go To Cell	Moves to any cell in a Worksheet.
Edit Cell	Modifies data in an individual cell in your Worksheet.

6. After making the changes in the worksheet, click on the Redraw button to see your changes appear in the chart without leaving the Chart Editor. Click on the Return button to exit the Chart Editor and return to the drawing window.

Changing the Chart Type

You can create eight data chart types in WP Presentations. Each is best suited for certain kinds of information. If you don't think the message conveyed by a particular chart is effective, try another chart type. To change the chart type, follow these steps:

1. Click on the Select tool located in the tool palette.

2. Double-click on the chart you want to change. This opens the Chart Editor. The Chart tool palette appears in the upper left side of the drawing window (see Figure 12.3).

3. Change the chart type by clicking on a chart icon in the Chart tool palette, or click on the Chart Gallery tool (see Figure 12.3). Click on the Chart Types button, and double-click on the chart type of your choice. The chart will be changed to reflect your choice.

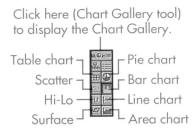

Click here (Chart Gallery tool)
to display the Chart Gallery.

Table chart — 　Pie chart
Scatter — 　Bar chart
Hi-Lo — 　Line chart
Surface — 　Area chart

Figure 12.3   Changing the chart type.

The Chart Gallery (see Figure 12.4), shows thumbnail sketches of up to 16 different chart styles, all variations of the current chart type. While in the Chart Gallery, you can also change the chart type. For example, you can change from a bar chart to a pie chart by clicking on the Chart Types button. A new Chart Gallery window will appear showing the thumbnail sketches of 12 chart types. Double-click on any of the sketches to select a new type.

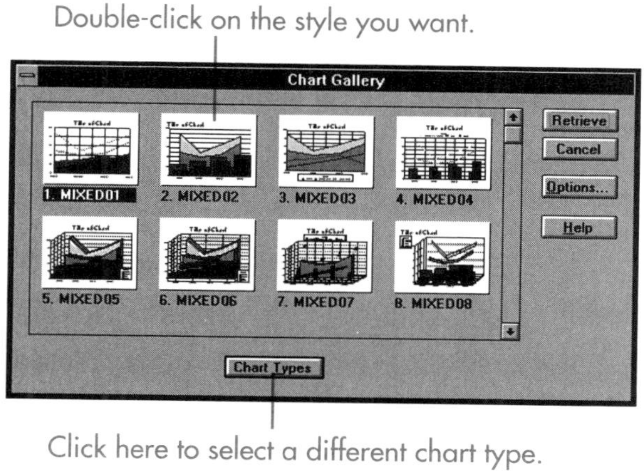

Double-click on the style you want.

Chart Gallery

Click here to select a different chart type.

Figure 12.4   Selecting Chart Styles and Types from the Chart
Gallery.

Importing Chart Data from Another Application

You can import all or part of a spreadsheet file into WP
Presentations so that you can create a data chart. WP Presentations supports the following spreadsheet programs:

Quattro Pro for Windows, Quattro, and Quattro Pro
(Versions 2.0–4.0)

Lotus 1-2-3 for Windows

Lotus 1-2-3 (Versions 2.01–3.1)

Microsoft Excel (Versions 2.1–4.0)

PlanPerfect (Versions 3.0–5.1)

Import   Import means to insert, add, or copy
data from a spreadsheet or text file created by
another application into the data chart worksheet.

Plain English

To import a spreadsheet into WP Presentations, follow these steps:

1. Open the Chart Editor by clicking on the Select tool in the tool palette and double-clicking on the chart.

2. Click on a worksheet cell where you want to begin importing the data from the spreadsheet.

3. Open the File menu, and click on Import or press F4. The Import Chart Data dialog box appears.

4. Enter the path and filename of the spreadsheet file (located on a floppy disk or your hard drive).

5. Click on the Import button. The Import Spreadsheet dialog box appears.

6. In the Range text box, specify the column and row numbers of the data you want to import. You will have to know the range in order to import the data. If the range you want to import has a range name, select the range you want to import from the Range Name list box.

7. Click on the Clear Current Data box to clear the current worksheet.

8. Click on the OK button. The new data appears in the WP Presentations' worksheet and the chart.

9. Click on the Return button to display the drawing window.

In this lesson, you learned the basics of creating data charts and how to import data from a spreadsheet program so you can create a chart of that data in WP Presentations. In the next lesson, you will learn how to enhance your data charts by adding titles, frames, and labels.

Lesson

Enhancing Charts

In this lesson, you will learn how to add titles, labels, and legends to your charts.

Adding Titles to Your Chart

An important element of a chart is the title. Chart titles are like headlines: they quickly introduce the reader to the chart's message. You can add a title, subtitle, and titles for each axis of your chart.

> **Axis** On many charts there are two axes. The X-axis is horizontal along the bottom of the chart, and the Y-axis is the vertical line along the left side of the chart. Axes are used to plot the data.

To add titles to your chart follow these steps:

1. Open the Chart Editor. If you need information on opening the Chart Editor, see Lesson 12.

2. Open the Options menu and click on Titles. The Titles dialog box appears (see Figure 13.1).

3. Type the title, subtitle, and axes titles in the text boxes.

4. Click on the OK button. The chart with your new titles appears.

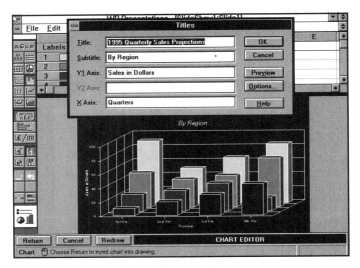

Figure 13.1   Adding titles to a chart.

Previewing Your Changes   Any time you make changes to your chart using the Options menu, you can preview the changes without leaving the dialog box by clicking on the Preview button.

Changing the Format of Chart Titles

There are three ways to change the format of your chart titles: You can change the positioning of chart titles, the fonts of the title text, and you can frame the titles of your charts in boxes.

There are three position options for your chart titles: left, center, or right. You can experiment to see what looks best for your chart.

The available fonts are the same as any other text used in your slide shows. If you need help on how to select text fonts, see Lesson 16.

If you want to put boxes around your chart titles you can choose from three styles: rectangle, rounded rectangle, or octagon. You can also change the color and border style of these boxes.

To format the titles of your charts, follow these steps:

1. Open the Chart Editor. If you need information on opening the Chart Editor, see Lesson 12.

2. Open the Options menu and click on Titles. The Titles dialog box appears.

3. If you haven't already done so, type the title, subtitle, and axes titles in the text boxes.

4. Click on the Options button. The Titles Options dialog box appears (see Figure 13.2).

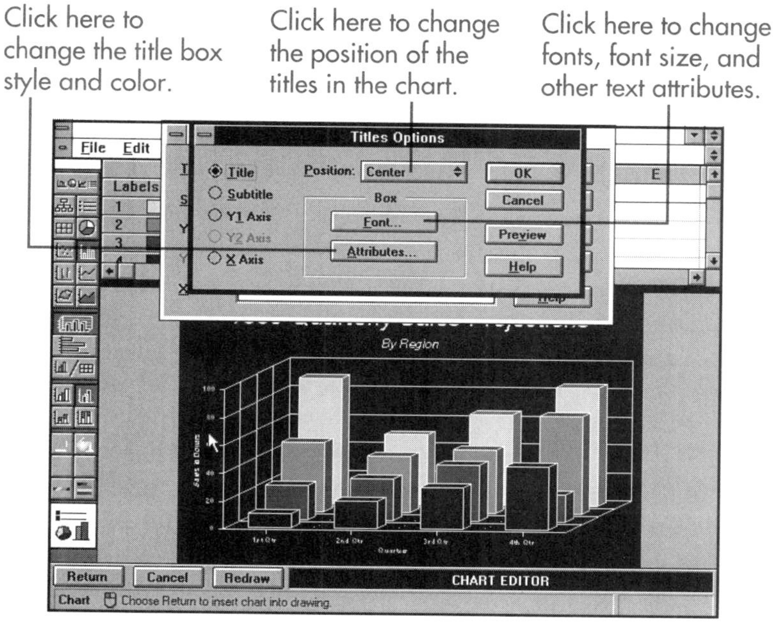

Click here to change the title box style and color.

Click here to change the position of the titles in the chart.

Click here to change fonts, font size, and other text attributes.

Figure 13.2   Formatting titles.

5. Click on the title (Chart title, subtitle, axes titles) you want to format.

6. To set the title position, click on the Position pop-up button and select either Left, Center, or Right.

7. To select a font as well as font size and other text attributes (underlining, italics, color, and so on) click on the Font button. If you need more help selecting text fonts, see Lesson 16.

8. To box-in your chart titles, click on the Attributes pop-up button. The Box Attributes dialog box appears. In that dialog box, you can choose the box style (rectangle, rounded rectangle, octagon, or None), color, and border style. For more information on formatting boxes, see Lesson 11, which shows how you can format the boxes in an organization chart.

9. After you have selected all your title formatting options, click on the OK button to close each dialog box until you return to the Chart Editor window.

Displaying Chart Labels

You can display the chart labels (which you assigned in the worksheet) in your data chart to enhance the message of the chart. Labels are text that show the numeric value, time period, or category of a bar, line, pie slice, or other item in a data chart. There are two methods for displaying chart labels in charts: one method displays labels on all the chart types except the pie charts, and the other method displays labels on pie charts only.

You'll learn how to display labels on all chart types in the next two sections.

Displaying Labels on All Chart Types Except Pie Charts

1. Open the Chart Editor. If you need information on opening the Chart Editor, see Lesson 12.

2. Open the Options menu and click on Labels. The Labels dialog box appears.

3. Click on Data Labels.

4. Click on the Display check box to display the labels on the chart. Click on the Preview button to see the effect of adding the labels to your chart. Take care not to make your chart look cluttered or confusing.

5. If you change your mind, you can click to uncheck the Display box, and the data labels will not appear on your chart.

6. Click on the Position pop-up list button, and select a position (below or above). You can choose to display the data labels above or below each related chart element.

7. Click on the OK button. The data labels appear on the graph.

Displaying Pie Chart Labels

Labels in a pie chart display the percent that each slice is of the whole pie and the numerical value of those pie pieces. Despite the fact that the pieces of pie in a pie chart are proportional in size, percentages are helpful labels because they show the exact measurements of the proportions. You can also add a leader line from the label to its piece of pie. Avoid creating "chart junk." Charts with chart junk have so many enhancements that the message becomes blurred.

Values, Percentages, Labels   In a pie chart, values are the worksheet numbers for each piece of the pie. Percentages are the proportions that each slice is of the whole pie. Labels are the worksheet descriptions of each slice.

To add the labels to a pie chart, follow these steps:

1. Open the Chart Editor. If you need information on opening the Chart Editor see Lesson 12.

2. Open the Options menu and click on Labels. The Pie Chart Labels dialog box appears (see Figure 13.3).

Figure 13.3   Adding labels, percentages, and values to a Pie Chart.

3. Click on the pop-up list buttons under Position to specify if you want to show values, percentages, and labels, and where you want to position each. You can choose to position the values, percentages, and labels either inside or outside the pie slices.

4. Under Orientation, click on either Vertical or Horizontal to specify whether you want the pie chart labels to be shown vertically or horizontally. The default selection is Horizontal, which works best in most cases.

5. When you display your information on the outside of the pie slice, use leaders to connect the data to the pie piece to which it belongs. Click on the Leader pop-up list to insert a line from an outside Value, Percent, and Label into the chart. The line can be of short, medium, or long length. You can experiment to determine which line length is best for your chart. The leader line will be inserted only for that data positioned outside the pie slice.

6. Click on the OK button. The labels appear on your pie chart.

> **Label Font**   If the font of your chart labels doesn't look right, don't panic. You can change Chart label fonts. By choosing Options Labels, you can click on the Font button to change both font and point size.

Displaying a Legend in a Chart

A chart *legend* identifies what each chart element represents. When you add a legend to a chart, it appears as a box that lists colors, patterns, or symbols used in the chart, and the related description of each. For example, if you are using a bar chart with the red bar representing the sales volume for the northern region, the legend will show the color red in a small box with the word *North*. To display a legend, follow these steps:

1. Open the Options menu and click on Legend. The Legend dialog box appears.

2. Select the Display Legend box by clicking it. The Display Legend box contains an **X** when selected.

3. Select from any of the following legend options:

Option	What It Does
Inside Chart	Positions the legend inside the chart.
Outside Chart	Positions the legend outside the chart.
Position	Positions the legend on one side or the other of the chart (top, middle, bottom).
Horizontal	Displays the chart legend horizontally.
Vertical	Displays the chart legend vertically.
Attributes	Determines the style, color, and border of the legend box.
Series Font	Determines the font type and size of the legend text.
Font	Determines the font type and size of the title text.

4. Click on the OK button. The legend appears in your chart.

In this lesson, you learned how to add titles and display labels and legends in your charts. In the next lesson, you will learn how to draw lines and shapes and how to edit, position, and resize them.

Lesson

Drawing Objects

In this lesson, you will learn how to draw lines and shapes and how to edit, position, and resize them.

Drawing Lines and Shapes

You can create your own artwork and include it on your slides. WP Presentations has a feature that allows you to draw objects and add them to your slides. You can draw any geometric shapes—rectangles, triangles, circles, or squares. You can also draw curved and straight lines and arrows, and WP Presentations has a freehand feature that lets you draw free-form shapes, polygons, and lines. All of these lines and shapes are *objects* in WP Presentations.

You can draw objects in the drawing window by clicking one of the drawing tools in the tool palette and using your mouse to create the line or shape. You may find drawing freehand objects with the mouse to be awkward and a little frustrating at first, but keep trying, and you'll find that practice does make perfect. Figure 14.1 shows the palette and identifies the drawing tools.

Drawing Window After selecting a drawing tool, the WP Presentations window becomes an area that you can draw in to create shapes and lines.

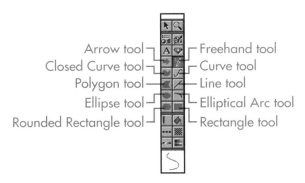

Arrow tool
Closed Curve tool
Polygon tool
Ellipse tool
Rounded Rectangle tool

Freehand tool
Curve tool
Line tool
Elliptical Arc tool
Rectangle tool

Figure 14.1 Drawing lines and shapes.

The procedure for drawing lines and shapes is basically the same no matter what you choose to draw. To draw lines and shapes follow these steps:

1. When you are in the drawing window, click on a drawing tool in the tool palette for the line or shape you want to draw (see figure 14.1).

2. Move the mouse pointer to where you want to begin drawing.

3. For geometric shapes and lines (not free-hand objects), click the left mouse button and drag the mouse pointer to begin drawing.

4. After you create the shape or line to the size you want, release the mouse button.

5. For drawing free-hand shapes and lines, click and drag the mouse to draw the shape you want. When you want to change directions, such as with a curve or an angle, click the mouse button again, and drag in the new direction.

Cancel a Drawing   If you start to draw and decide you want to back out, press Esc.

6. Double-click to finish drawing a free-hand shape or line.

7. To reposition a drawing, press the right mouse button and drag the drawing to a new location.

Editing Objects

Editing an object involves changing its line style and color, and its fill pattern and color. You can fill closed objects, such as a rectangle or circle, with a pattern and color. To work with a shape or line that you've already drawn, you must first select it using the Select tool in the Tool palette.

Pattern   A pattern is a design you can put inside an object. For example, rather than have the inside of a rectangle a solid color, you can fill it with a checkerboard pattern.

To edit an object, follow these steps:

1. Select the object by clicking on the Select tool in the tool palette. Click on the object. You will know you selected it if handles (small squares) appear around the object.

2. Click on one of the Edit Object tools, as shown in Figure 14.2.

3. To change a line style, click on the Line Pattern tool, and in the pop-up box, click on the line thickness and style you want. The line thickness and style of the line you have selected changes.

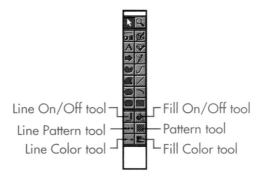

Line On/Off tool
Line Pattern tool
Line Color tool

Fill On/Off tool
Pattern tool
Fill Color tool

Figure 14.2 Editing an object.

4. To change the line color, click and hold down the mouse button on the Line Color tool while you select one of the colors in the pop-up palette.

5. To change the pattern, click on the Fill Color Pattern tool and click on the pattern you want. The pattern in the selected object changes.

6. To change the color that fills the shape, click and hold down the mouse button on the Fill Color tool while you select one of the colors in the pop-up color palette. The color in the selected shape changes.

> **Selecting More Than One Object** To select more than one object at a time, click on the Select tool and hold down the Ctrl key while dragging the mouse pointer to encompass the objects in a dashed line.

Arranging Objects

Once you have created your objects in the drawing window, you may want to move them to different locations for a more balanced look. To arrange objects in the drawing window, you can move them around with the mouse.

To move an object:

1. Select the object by clicking on the Select tool in the tool palette. Click on the object. Handles (small squares that surround the object when you selected it) appear around the object.

2. Click on the object and drag it to its new location. When you have the object repositioned, release the mouse button.

Sizing Objects

You may want to change the size of some of your objects so they fit on the drawing window better. To change the size of an object:

1. Select the object by clicking on the Select tool in the tool palette. Click on the object. Handles (small squares) appear around the object.

2. Position the mouse pointer over a handle until it becomes a double-headed arrow.

3. Click and drag the handle until the shape becomes the size you want and then release the mouse button. Click the corner handle to keep the sides of the object proportional.

In this chapter, you learned how to draw objects (lines and shapes) and how to edit and arrange those objects on a slide. In the next lesson, you will learn how to work with colors and backgrounds to enhance your slides.

Lesson

Working with Background Colors

In this lesson, you will learn how to select solid background colors and gradient background colors for your slides. You will also learn how to change the style of the gradient background on your slides.

Selecting a Background Color

When you work with slide show masters to create your slides, the background color of the slides is preset. There are many different slide show masters, and you will probably find one that has a color to fit your needs. However, if you don't see what you want, you can choose your own background color for your slides. You have two choices: you can choose a new background color for just the current slide that you are working on, or you can set a default to change the background for all the new slides you create. You can only change the background colors when you are working with the No Template template. Also, the slide colors that you choose can be solid colors or a blend of two colors, which is called a *gradient*.

Slide Show Masters A slide show master is a predesigned slide that serves as the backdrop or foundation of the entire slide show. For example, in the slide show master called City, each slide has a city skyline as its background.

Plain English

Selecting a Solid Background Color for the Current Slide

You can select one of 256 colors for your slide. WP Presentations refers to the background of a slide as a *page*. Therefore, to select a slide color, you use the Page Layout command that is found in the File menu. To select a background color for the currently displayed slide, follow these steps:

1. Click on the template pop-up list button at the bottom of the WP Presentations Window and select No Template. The drawing window changes to a white background.

2. Open the File menu, and click on Page Layout. The Page Layout dialog box appears (see Figure 15.1).

Click here for a solid color background.

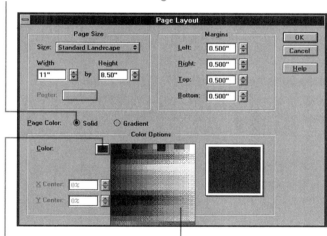

Click on the Color palette to   Color palette
select the background color.

Figure 15.1   Selecting background colors.

3. Click on the Solid option for Page Color.

4. Click on the Color palette and hold the mouse button to select a color of your choice. The new background color appears in a box on the right side of the Color Options group box.

5. Click on the OK button. Your current slide appears with the new background color.

Solid Colors   There are 256 colors in the background palette, and although WP Presentations refers to the color option as solid, some of the colors are not really solid but are a colorized pattern, such as small diamonds or dots. If you want to use a completely solid color in your background, choose from one of the 16 colors in the top row of the Color palette.

Selecting a Default Color for All New Slides

If you want all the new slides in your slide show to have the same solid color for a background, you need to change one of the defaults of WP Presentations. To change the background color default, follow these steps:

Defaults   Initial settings that WP Presentations will automatically use until you specify an alternative.

1. Open the File menu, and click on Preferences. The Preferences dialog box appears (see Figure 15.2).

2. Double-click on the Page Layout icon. The Page Layout dialog box appears (see Figure 15.1).

Figure 15.2   Changing the background color default setting.

3. Click on the Solid option for Page Color.

4. Click on the Color palette and hold the mouse button to select a color. The color that will be used as a default for all new slides appears in a box on the right side of the Color Options group box.

5. Click on the OK button. The Update Page Settings dialog box appears with the prompt, **Do you want the current document to be updated with new page settings?** Click on Yes. The background color changes and the Preferences dialog box appears. Click on Close to close the dialog box.

The background color will be set to your choice for all new slides that you create in this document until you change the color setting by following the above steps.

Selecting Gradient Background Colors for a Slide

Rather than use one solid color for a slide background, you can use a *gradient background*. A gradient background is a gradual blending of two colors. To create a gradient background, follow these steps:

1. To create a gradient background for the current slide only, open the File menu, and click on Page Layout. The Page Layout dialog box appears (see Figure 15.1).

2. Click on Gradient for the Page Color (if it is not already selected).

3. Select a Center Color and an Outer Color from the Color palette in the Color Options group box. These will be the two colors that will be gradually blended together on your slide. The center color is the top color that gradually blends to become the outer color. The color gradients appear in a box on the right of the Color Options group box.

4. Click on the OK button. Your slide appears with the new gradient colors.

5. If you want to choose a default set of gradient background colors to appear on all new slides you create, choose Preferences from the File menu and double-click on the Page Layout icon to display the Page Layout dialog box. Follow steps 1–3.

6. Click on the OK button. The Update Page Settings dialog box appears with the prompt, **Do you want the current document to be updated with new page settings?** Click on Yes. The background color changes and the Preferences dialog box appears. Click on Close to close the dialog box.

Changing the Gradient Background Style of a Slide

When you choose a gradient background, you are using a two-color background in which the colors are gradually blended together. You can change the design of that blend to give different special effects. For example, you can choose to have a linear gradient blend that flows from the top to the bottom of the slide with the color changing from the first color (called the center color) to the second color (called the outer color). You can choose a circular or a rectangular gradient, both of which are described later in this lesson.

You can also control how gradually the colors will blend by using either of two blending options: Auto-step blending or Fixed blending. Auto-step blending uses the maximum number of steps possible when blending the colors and results in a more gradual transition from one color to another. The Fixed blending option allows you to select the number of blend steps you want to see between the center and the outer colors. The effect of the two options is quite different and something you should experiment with. To change the gradient background of a slide, follow these steps:

1. To change the gradient style for the current slide only, open the File menu and click on Page Layout. The Page Layout dialog box appears (see Figure 15.1).

2. If you want to change the gradient background for all future slides (that is, change the default gradient blend), choose Preferences from the File menu, and choose Page Layout. The Page Layout dialog box appears.

3. Click on Gradient for the Page Color (if it is not already selected).

4. If you haven't already done so, select a Center Color and an Outer Color from the Color palette in the Color Options group box.

5. Click on the Type pop-up list, and hold the mouse button down to select one of the following choices:

Linear   Colors blend from top to bottom.

Circular   Colors blend out from the center in a round shape.

Rectangular   Colors blend out from the center in a rectangular shape.

6. If you want the blending of the two colors to be as gradual as possible, select Auto-step Blending.

7. If you want to control the number of blend steps between the center and outside colors, select Fixed and enter the number of blend steps (gradation of color) you want in the Fixed box. For example, if you enter the number 3, you will have the center color, the shade that results from mixing the two colors, and the outer color. The new gradient style appears in a box on the right side of the Color Options group box.

8. Click on the OK button. Your current slide appears with the new color gradient style.

9. If you changed gradient styles using Preferences, choose Yes, and choose Close to close the Preferences dialog box.

In this lesson, you learned how to change the solid and gradient background colors of your slide. In the next lesson, you will learn how to change the colors and other attributes of text.

Lesson

Enhancing Text

In this lesson, you will learn how to change the format of your text by changing fonts, and how to add emphasis by adding boldface, italics, underlining, and color.

Making Text Format Changes

If you work with a word processing program or spreadsheet software, then you know about text formatting. When you format text, you change its appearance. You change the font style and size, or you make the text bold, italic, or underlined.

You make all text format changes by using the Font dialog box, so making changes is very easy. Text format changes must be made to each slide individually—you can't make any changes to all the slides at once. Although you use the Font dialog box for all the format changes, how you get to that dialog box is different depending on whether the text you want to change was created using the Outliner (Lesson 4) or the Text Tool (Lesson 5). In this lesson, you will learn about both methods for changing text formats.

Changing Fonts and Text Appearance

You can choose from several font types and sizes for your text, and each will change how the audience interprets the message of your slides. Large, plain fonts may present a serious, important message, whereas script fonts may be more appropriate for conveying lighter, more creative or artistic messages. You also can change the basic appearance of your text by making the text bold or italic or by underlining it. Each of these three basic appearance changes can add emphasis to your text. To change the font and text appearance, follow these steps:

Font A font is a group of letters, numbers, and symbols with a common typeface. For example, Times Roman 12-point describes the font by name and size.

1. If you created your text using the Outliner, open the Outliner window by clicking on the Outliner button at the bottom of the screen. The outline of the slide appears in the upper portion of the screen. The status bar at the bottom of the screen indicates that you are in the Chart Editor. Select the text you want to change by dragging the mouse over the text to highlight it.

2. If you created your text using the Text tool from the tool palette, click on the Select tool, and double-click on the text object (a text line or text area) you want to change. The text line or text area will open. Select the text you want to change by dragging the mouse over the text to highlight it.

Text Line or Text Area Text that you add to a slide by using the Text Tool will appear in a box-like area called a *text line* or *text area*. This type of text is an object, which means that you can format, move, and edit the text in the same manner as other objects (drawings, charts, and so on).

3. Once you select the text, open the Text menu and click on Font. The Font dialog box appears (see Figure 16.1).

Sample text

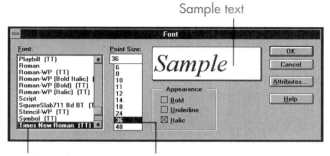

Click on a font choice.   Click on a point size.

Figure 16.1 Changing fonts.

Shortcut Key You can display the Font dialog box by selecting the text and pressing F9.

4. Select a font from the Font list box by clicking on your choice. A sample of the font you select will appear in the sample text of the dialog box.

5. Select a font size from the Point Size list box by clicking on a size.

6. In the Appearance group box, select or deselect any of the three choices (Bold, Underline, or Italic) by clicking in the check box. An **X** indicates you have selected the feature.

Shortcut Text Formatting Keys You can quickly add bold, underlining, or italic to your text by selecting the text and pressing Ctrl+B for bold, Ctrl+U for underlining, or Ctrl+I for italics. To turn off any of these three types of formatting, press Ctrl+N.

7. Click on the OK button. If you created your text using the Text tool, you return to the slide and the font changes appear.

8. If you are in the Chart Editor (text created using the Outliner), you will return to the Chart Editor. Click on the Redraw button at the bottom of the screen to see the font changes. Click on the Return button at the bottom of the screen to exit the Chart Editor.

Changing the Color of Text

You can outline text like other objects, and fill it with a color or pattern. The fill color and pattern are inside the outline of the letters. For example, you can fill the inside of your text with pink polka dots. You can also have gradient colors in your text, similar to the gradient colors used in your background (see Lesson 15).

Follow these steps to change the color of text:

1. Select the text you want to add color and/or a pattern to. See the above section for details on selecting text.

2. Open the Text menu and click on Font. The Font dialog box appears (see Figure 16.1).

3. Click on the Attributes button. The Text Attributes dialog box appears.

4. Click Pattern, Gradient, or None. Pattern fills letters with a solid color or pattern (see Lesson 15). Gradient fills letters with a blend of two colors. If you choose None, the text will not be filled with any color but will appear as an outline.

5. If you choose Pattern, click one or more of the following options:

Foreground Color   Changes the color for the pattern.

Background Color   Changes the color behind the pattern.

Pattern   Changes the pattern within the text.

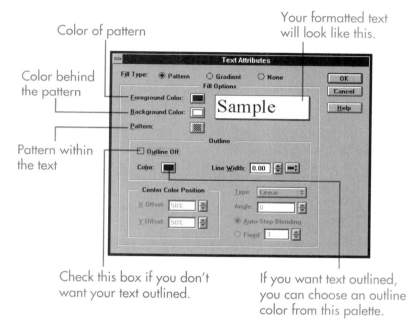

Figure 16.2   Changing Text Color.

6. If you choose Gradient, click one of the following options:

Center Color   Changes the center color for circular and rectangular designs, or changes the top color linear gradients.

Outer Color   Changes the outer color for circular and rectangular designs; or change the bottom color for linear gradients.

Outline Off   Removes the outline of text.

7. To change the gradient type, click on the Type arrow button to select linear, circular, or rectangular. To change the default Auto-step blend to Fixed, select Fixed and enter the number of step changes you want from the center to the outer color.

8. Click on the OK button to close the Attributes dialog box.

9. Click on the OK button to close the Font dialog box. If you created your text using the Text Tool, you return to the slide and the new text color changes appear.

10. If you are in the Chart Editor (text created using the Outliner), you return to the Chart Editor. Click on the Redraw button at the bottom of the screen to see the text color changes. Click on the Return button at the bottom of the screen to exit the Chart Editor.

In this lesson, you learned how to enhance text by adding emphasis in the form of bold, underlining, and italics and how to color the text. In the next lesson, you learn how to spell check and search through your text.

Lesson 17

Spell Check and Text Search

In this lesson, you will learn how to check your slides for misspelled words and how to search and replace text.

Checking for Misspellings

WP Presentations has a spell checker called The WordPerfect Speller. It's the same feature found in other WordPerfect software, and if you've used other spell checkers, you'll find it easy to use. With the Speller, you can check any text you add to a slide, including text in a text object (a text line or text area created with the Text tool—Lesson 5), and text in the slide show outline (created with the Outliner—Lesson 4). The Speller also identifies two consecutive occurrences of a word and capitalization errors.

The Speller does have one drawback: it doesn't allow you to globally check the spelling of all text in all text objects in the slide show at once. For text that you enter using the Text tool, you must spell check every text line and area individually. That is not the case with text created using the Outliner. You can check the spelling of all the text in the Outliner with one action.

To check for misspelled words in your slide show, follow these steps:

1. If you created the text using the Text tool (that is, a text object, either a text line or text area), click on the Select tool and double-click in the text line or area. The text object opens.

2. If you created the text using the Outliner, click on the Outliner button at the bottom of the screen. You are now in the Outliner view.

3. If you want to spell check all the words in the text object or outline, place the insertion point anywhere in the text. If you only want to check the spelling of one word or a group of words within the text object or outline, highlight the text by dragging the mouse over it.

4. Open the Text menu and click on Speller.

5. Click on the Start button. The Speller dialog box appears (see Figure 17.1).

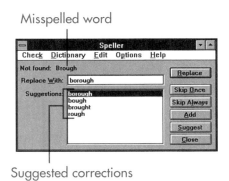

Misspelled word

Suggested corrections

Figure 17.1 Checking the spelling of your text.

6. When the Speller finds an incorrectly spelled word, it highlights the word and suggests a replacement in the Replace With text box. Additional suggested replacements appear in the Suggestions list box. To accept the text shown in the Replace With box, click on the Replace button. To select one of the words in the Suggestions list, click on the choice and click on the Replace button. You can also click one of the following options:

Skip Once   Skips the misspelled word; detects its next occurrence.

Skip Always   Skips every occurrence of the word.

Add   Adds the word to the dictionary.

7. Click on Close to exit Speller. The Speller saves the corrections you have made. If you are in the Chart Editor, click on the Redraw button at the bottom to display the corrected text. Click on the Return button to exit the Outliner.

Shortcut Keys   To quickly display the Speller dialog box, press Ctrl+F1.

Finding and Replacing Text

You may find the search feature helpful if you want to quickly find a word or phrase in the Outliner in order to edit or reformat it (change its color, font, and other attributes). This feature is also very helpful and convenient when you want to replace or edit every occurrence of specific text. For example, if you used the word "partnership" in several of your slides and you want to replace it with the word "corporation," you can make a global replacement with one command.

Searching Text Objects The search and replace function for text objects does not have the global capabilities that the Outliner has. You can only search the text in each selected text object and cannot search through all text objects in a slide show at once.

Searching for Text

To search for a word or phrase, follow these steps:

1. Open the text object or Outliner that contains the text that you want to search through.

2. Position the insertion point where you want WP Presentations to start the search.

3. Open the Text menu and click on Search/Replace. The Search and Replace dialog box appears (see Figure 17.2).

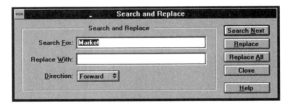

Figure 17.2 Searching for text.

Shortcut Key Press F2 to quickly display the Search and Replace dialog box.

4. In the Search For text box, enter the word or phase that you want to find.

5. If you want to search forward in the text object or Outliner, make sure that the Direction pop-up button shows Forward. If you want the search to go backward from the insertion point, click on the Direction pop-up list button and select Backward.

6. Click on the Search Next button. WP Presentations will find the next occurrence of the search text and highlight it.

7. When WP Presentations finds the text, you can click on the Close button to perform the editing or formatting, or click on Search Next to find the next occurrence of the search text.

Replacing Text

You can have WP Presentations search for a word or phrase and replace one or all instances of the word or phrase.

To search and replace text, follow these steps:

1. Open the text object or Outliner that contains the text you want to search through.

2. Position the insertion point where you want WP Presentations to start the search.

3. Open the Text menu and click on Search/Replace. The Search and Replace dialog box appears (see Figure 17.2).

4. In the Search For text box, enter the word or phrase you want to replace.

5. Tab down to the Replace With text box and type the new text (replacement text).

6. Click on the Direction pop-up list button and select Forward or Backward. Forward searches from the insertion point forward; Backward searches from the insertion point backward.

7. If you want to replace all instances of the text in one immediate action, click on Replace All. If you want to decide whether to replace each occurrence of the text, click on the Search Next button. When you want to make the replacement, click on the Replace button.

> **Shortcut to Delete All Instances of Text**   To delete all occurrences of text in a text object or outline, follow the same steps for replacing text, but instead of entering a replacement text in the Replace With text box of the Search and Replace dialog box, leave the text box blank.

In this lesson, you learned how to check your slides for misspelled words and how to search for and replace words and phrases. In the next lesson, you'll learn how to create special transitions from one slide to the next in your slide shows.

Creating Transitions from Slide to Slide

In this lesson, you will learn how to control the way you move from one slide to another in a slide show, and how to allow viewers of a slide show to easily jump to slides that are not in sequential order.

Choosing Screen Wipes

To move from one slide to another when you are playing a slide show, you perform a *slide transition* or a *screen wipe*. The default way that WP Presentations moves from one slide to another is to simply replace the current slide with the next slide of the slide show. This default is the *normal* transition. You can use ten other types of transitions: Wipe, Open, Close, Box, Spots, Blinds, Jigsaw, Snake, Diagonal, and Overwrite. These different transition types break up the monotony of a presentation and add a touch of professionalism to your slide show.

The names of most of these transitions explain how they look. For example, the Jigsaw transition makes the transition from one slide to the next by filling in the slide with shapes that look like pieces of a jigsaw puzzle. Likewise, the Blinds transition moves you from one slide to the next in a way that looks like window blinds closing. Other transitions are more difficult to explain but you can preview them.

To choose a type of transition, follow these steps:

1. Open an existing slide show or create one.

2. Open the Slide menu and click on Transition. The Slide Transition dialog box opens (see Figure 18.1).

Click on arrows to select the
slide you want to transition to.

Figure 18.1   Creating slide transitions.

3. Click the arrow buttons to select the slide that you want to add the transition effect to. For example, if you want to change the transition from slide 2 to slide 3 from Normal to Jigsaw, click the arrow buttons to select slide number 3.

4. Click on the pop-up list button, and select a transition type. If you choose any transition other than Normal and Overwrite, either the Direction or Size pop-up list button appears. Click on that button and select an appropriate direction or size. The direction you choose determines which way the screen will "wipe" away the current slide and display the next one. The size will determine how large the transition effect will appear on the screen.

5. Repeat steps 3 and 4 to specify the type of transition you want between all the other slides in the show.

6. Click on the OK button. You return to your slide show.

7. To view your transitions, click on the Slide menu and select Play Slide Show (see Lesson 8 for more information).

Previewing Transitions

You may have to experiment a little to get the right type of transition for each slide. A transition may seem like a good idea, but when you run the show, it may not "fit" your presentation. Also, not all the transition type names are self-explanatory. You may not be able to visualize transitions from names like Box, Wipe, Spots, and Snake. One way to experiment with slide transitions—to see what they look like—is to choose one and preview it while still in the Slide Transitions dialog box. To preview a transition, follow these steps:

1. Select a slide transition type and direction by following steps 1 through 4 in the previous section.

2. Click on the Preview button in the Slide Transition dialog box. The slide transition preview appears in a small window at the top right of the Slide Transition dialog box.

3. Click on the arrows in the Slide Transition dialog box to move from one slide to another. As you click to move to another slide, WP Presentations demonstrates the transition in the Preview Transition window.

   After the transition plays, press Esc to continue working in the Slide Transition dialog box.

4. Click on the OK button to exit the Slide Transition dialog box.

Creating Slide Links

Sometimes in a presentation, you may not want to view the
slides in sequential order. You may want to jump to slides
out of order to emphasize specific points to your audience.
You can do this by creating links between these slides. You
link related slides together by assigning Go To keys. These
Go To keys are keyboard numbers or letters that the viewer
of the slide show can press to jump to a specific slide of
related information. This type of linking gives the slide show
an interactive feature.

For example, on a slide you can show information
about a particular supplier of merchandise; on that slide you
can instruct the user to "Press key 1 for the address and
phone number of this supplier" if they want the address and
phone number of the supplier. When they press 1, the slide
show will jump to the slide that contains the address and
phone number.

To create slide show links, follow these steps:

1. Open an existing slide show or create one.

2. Open the Slide menu and click on Slide Links. The
Slide Links dialog box appears (see Figure 18.2).

Figure 18.2 Linking slides.

3. Click the arrow buttons to select the slide you want to jump from.

4. In the Key text box, enter the letter or number that you want to assign as the Go To key. This is what you will instruct users to press to jump to a related slide.

5. In the Go to Slide drop-down list box, click on the number of the slide that you want to jump to.

6. Click on the Add button to assign the Go To key. The Go To key assignment appears in the Key list box.

7. Continue to add more Go To keys by following steps 2 through 6.

8. When you have created all the links you want, click on the OK button. You return to your slide show.

9. To review your slide links, play your slide show. Click on the Slide menu and select Play Slide Show.

10. Make any changes necessary in the Play Slide Show dialog box, and select Play.

11. When the slide to which you assigned the Go to Number appears, press the assigned number to jump to that slide.

Slide Linking Works Only with Manual Advance The slide linking feature will only work if you set the slide show on Manual Advance. You can set it to manual by choosing Slide Transition and clicking on Manual in the Advance box.

In this lesson, you learned how to move from one slide to another using the special transition effects of WP Presentations and how to link slides so that you can jump from one slide to another related slide.

Lesson

19

Displaying an Overview of a Slide Show

In this lesson, you will learn how to display your slides in a list that gives an overview of the slide show. You will also learn how to use the Slide List to arrange slides and change slide options.

Viewing the Slide List

You've created a slide show in preparation for the big marketing meeting tomorrow. To further prepare yourself, you have shown a "dry-run" of your presentation to some of your peers. They've made some suggestions, such as rearranging the order of your information, changing some of the transition effects, and making a few changes to wording and formatting. You now need to make these changes as quickly as possible. WP Presentations has a feature that will help you do just that: the Slide List. The Slide List feature shows you summary information about each slide, which allows you to take a quick look at the slide show layout and all the options you have chosen for each slide. Using the Slide List, you can quickly rearrange your slides and even access them to make changes, if necessary. To view the Slide List, follow these steps:

1. Open or create a slide show.

2. Click on the Slide List button located at the bottom of the WP Presentations window. The Slide List appears (see Figure 19.1). You can also display the Slide List by opening the View menu and clicking and holding the mouse button on Slide Show to select List.

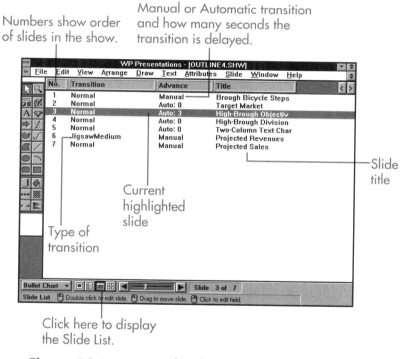

Figure 19.1   Viewing the Slide List.

Changing the Order of Slides

You can use the Slide List to rearrange the order of the slides in the slide show. For example, if you want to move the second slide in your show to the last position, you can make that move while in the Slide List window by following these steps:

1. Open the Slide List window by following the steps in the preceding section.

2. Select the slide that you want to move by clicking on it. When you select a slide in the Slide List window, you will highlight the entire row of information.

Deleting a Slide While in the Slide List, you can delete a slide by selecting it and pressing Del.

3. Drag the selected slide to the new position. When you get the slide into position, release the mouse button. A colored line will underline the slide position so that you will know when you have reached the desired location. The *position line* is a temporary guide line that will remain on screen until you release the mouse button.

Accessing a Slide If you want to access a particular slide to display or edit it, double-click on that slide, and it will appear. When you finish, click on the Slide List button to return to the Slide List.

Customizing the Slide List

The initial setup of WP Presentations has four columns of information in the Slide List Heading bar: Number, Title,

Transition, and Advance. When you are making changes to your slide show within the Slide List, you may find you need additional information displayed about your slides to make some final decisions. You can customize the Slide List Heading bar by adding, deleting, or moving columns of information.

Adding and Deleting Columns of Information to the Slide List

You may want to add or delete information displayed about your slides on the Slide List Heading bar.

To add or delete columns of information in the Slide List, follow these steps:

1. Move the mouse pointer onto any blank space on the Heading bar either between existing columns or at the end of all the columns on the Heading bar. The color between the columns and at the ends of the Heading bar is different than the columns themselves.

2. Press the right mouse button to display the Quick menu, as shown in Figure 19.2.

3. The Quick menu displays in darker type those items that are not yet column headings. The four items that are not part of the initial default headings are

   Template   Lists the template used for the slide.

   Controls   Indicates whether the slide is linked to another slide.

   Notes   Indicates if the slide has speaker notes.

   Sound   Lists the types of sound files, if any, used in the slide.

Heading bar   Slide List quick menu

Figure 19.2 Adding additional information to the Slide List.

4. Select the item from the Quick menu that you want to include as an information column in the Slide List. The item appears in the Heading bar, and the related information for each slide in your slide show automatically appears.

5. To remove one of the columns of information from the Heading bar, click and drag the column off the bar.

> **Running Out of Space**   If you run out of space on the Heading bar and you want to add more items, I'll tell you how to resize your columns in the "Moving and Resizing Columns" section.

Moving and Resizing Columns

To rearrange the order of the columns, and to resize them using the Slide List, follow these steps:

1. Move the mouse pointer onto the column heading that you want to move.

2. Click and hold down the left mouse button, and drag the column heading into the new position.

3. Release the mouse button.

4. To resize the columns, move the mouse to either the left or right outer edge of the column you want to resize. The pointer changes to a double-headed arrow. Click and drag the edge of the column to shrink or expand its size.

5. If you want to save your new arrangement, open the File menu and click on Preferences.

6. Double-click on the Environment icon. The Environment dialog box appears (see Figure 19.3).

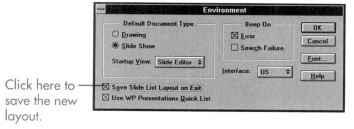

Click here to save the new layout.

Figure 19.3 Saving the new arrangement of columns in the Slide List.

7. Click on the Save Slide List Layout on Exit check box.

8. Click on the OK button. The Preferences dialog box appears.

9. Click on the Close button. When you exit the slide show, WP Presentations saves the new arrangement of columns.

Changing Slide Options Using the Slide List

Each column of information in the Slide List shows options, settings, and features of every slide in your slide show. You can use this list to quickly open the dialog box that contains the settings related to that column heading. For example, from the Slide List, you can open the Slide Order, Slide Title, and Slide Transition dialog boxes, to name a few. This is a quick way to change slide options while in the Slide List. To use column headings to open the dialog boxes, follow these steps:

1. Select a slide by clicking on its row.

2. Move the mouse pointer to the column slide information in the row that represents a setting, option, or feature that you want to change.

3. With the right mouse button, click once.

4. The related dialog box opens. Make your changes and close the dialog box to return to the Slide List.

In this lesson, you learned how to view your slide show in a list format called the Slide List. You learned how to change the order of your slides, customize the Slide List, and make changes to your charts within the Slide List. In the next lesson, you will learn how to become efficient with WP Presentations by creating and editing the Button Bars.

Lesson

20

Working with Button Bars

In this lesson, you will learn how to change the position of the Button Bar, how to create your own Button Bar, and how to edit existing Button Bars.

Changing the Position and Style of the Button Bar

In Lesson 2, you learned the basics of using the WP Presentations Button Bars. The Button Bars are rows of buttons that you can click to carry out tasks, such as saving a file, adding a slide, and playing a slide show. Using Button Bars saves time. They are a much faster and more intuitive way of performing tasks than using the menu bar to click and select items. If you like using the mouse, Button Bars are faster than using the shortcut keys.

You can position the Button Bar at the top of the screen, or at the left, right, or bottom. You may find one position more efficient for you to access than other positions; experiment to see what is best for you. The default position of the Button Bar is at the top of the screen. You also can change the style of the buttons. The default style is a combination of text and pictures. If you change the style to only text or only pictures (icons), you can fit more buttons on the screen at one time. To change the position and style, follow these steps:

1. Display the Button Bar. For information on how to select and display a Button Bar, see Lesson 2.

2. Open the View menu, click on Button Bar Setup, and then click on Options. The Button Bar Options dialog box appears (see Figure 20.1).

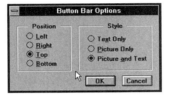

Figure 20.1   Changing the position of the Button Bar.

3. Click on the position you want for your Button Bars in the drawing window.

4. Click on a style for your Button Bars. You can display buttons that have only text, only pictures (icons) on the buttons, or both picture and text on the buttons. The picture and text setting shows larger buttons. If you choose that option, you may not be able to see all the buttons at one time on the Button Bar. To maximize the number of buttons you can see on the Button Bar, position the buttons on the left or right side of the WP Presentations window and use the Text only button style.

5. Click on the OK button. The new Button Bar style and location appears in the drawing window.

Creating Your Own Button Bar

There are 11 predefined Button Bars for you to select from (see Lesson 2). The buttons on the Button Bars represent menu selections from the menu bar that you're most likely to

use; however, you can also create customized Button Bars
that will contain only those buttons you want to use to meet
your specific needs. When you create a customized Button
Bar, you are, in essence, adding menu items to a Button Bar.
To create a Button Bar, follow these steps:

1. Open the View menu, click on Button Bar Setup,
and then click on New. The Edit Button Bar dialog
box appears (see Figure 20.2).

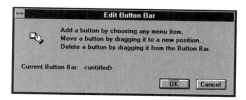

Figure 20.2 Creating a Button Bar.

2. From the menu bar at the top of the screen, open
menus, and click on the menu items that you want
to add to the Button Bar. As you click on menu
items, their buttons are added to the Button Bar tray
in the WP Presentations window (as shown in
Figure 20.3). You can add as many buttons as you
like to your new Button Bar. If you fill up the whole
Button Bar space in the WP Presentations window,
Button Bar scroll arrows appear so you can scroll to
those buttons that are not visable.

Scroll   To scroll means to advance—like
flipping through the pages of a book. You
advance through them, displaying one after
another. If you are scrolling through the buttons on
a Button Bar, you display those buttons that you
can't currently see.

The new buttons appear
on the Button Bar tray.

Click the menu item that you
want to add to the Button Bar.

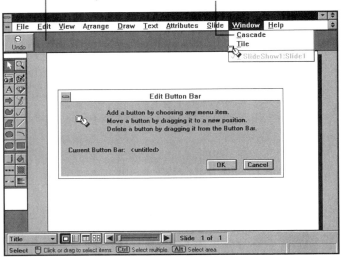

Figure 20.3   Adding buttons to the Button Bar.

3. When you finish adding buttons, click on the OK
button. The Save Button Bar dialog box appears.

4. Enter a name for the new Button Bar in the Save As
text box. This is the file name for your newly
created Button Bar. WP Presentations adds a .PRB
extension to the file name. Click on Save and your
new Button Bar appears.

Editing a Button Bar

You can make changes to any Button Bar, including any of
the predefined bars or any that you create. By editing a
Button Bar, you can add and delete a few buttons and quickly
create a bar to meet your special needs. You can add, delete,
and move buttons by following these steps:

1. Select a Button Bar by opening the View menu and
clicking on Button Bar Setup; then click on Select.
The Select Button Bar dialog box appears (see
Figure 20.4).

> **Select Button Bar**   To quickly change Button
> Bars, right-click on the Button Bar and select a
> different Button Bar.

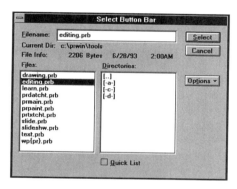

Figure 20.4   Selecting a Button Bar.

2. Enter the filename of the Button Bar you want to
select in the Filename text box, or click on the
Button Bar file name in the Files list box.

> **Editing a Button Bar**   If you edit one of the
> predefined Button Bars and you want to save it for
> future use, don't save it using the same name as
> the original Button Bar. By choosing a different
> name, you will still have the original Button Bar available
> if you need it.

3. Choose Select. The Button Bar appears in the
drawing window.

4. Open the View menu again, click on Button Bar Setup, and click on Edit. The Edit Button Bar dialog box appears (see Figure 20.2).

5. To add a button, click on the menu item of your choice, as describe in the preceding section of this lesson.

6. To move a button to new position on the bar, click and drag the button to its new location on the Button Bar. Be sure to keep it on the Button Bar. If you drag it off the bar and release the mouse, you will delete the button, as described in step 7.

7. To delete a button from the Button Bar, click and drag it completely off the Button Bar and release the mouse button.

> **Deleting a Button by Mistake**   If you delete a button by mistake, you can't undo the deletion by choosing Edit Undo. By choosing Edit Undo, you will add the Undo button to the Button Bar. To get a deleted button back onto the Button Bar, add it back by following the steps described in this lesson.

In this lesson, you learned how to move, create, and edit Button Bars. In the next lesson, you will learn how to add sounds to your slides from your CDs or sound files.

Lesson

Adding Sound to Slides

In this lesson, you will learn how to add MIDI, digital audio, and CD audio sounds and music to your slides.

Sound Basics

WP Presentations allows you to create a multimedia presentation by adding sounds to your slides. The sound can be music, special effects, or if you have the necessary equipment, your voice; however, to play sound, you will need PC speakers and a sound card. To record sound, you also will need a PC microphone. There are three types of sound clips that you can add to your slide show: MIDI (Musical Digital Interface), digital audio, and CD.

> **Sound Clips** Files that contain music, voice, or special effects that you can play through your PC's speakers. To play sound clips, you will need a sound device, such as a sound board and stereo-like speakers. If the sound files are on CD, you will also need a CD-ROM player for your PC.

MIDI files are a re-creation of musical sounds. They are not a recording of the sounds; they're files that contain instructions that tell your PC how to imitate a musical sound and other special effects. WP Presentations comes with over 100 MIDI sound files that you can use. These sound clips include jazz and classical music, and special effects such as a bird chirping, the ocean, and a phone ringing.

Digital audio files are more like tape recordings and have a higher-quality, more realistic sound than MIDI files. These higher-quality sounds create larger files, which take up more disk space than the MIDI files. If you have a PC microphone, you can record sounds and save them in a digital audio file. However, recording sounds for your WP Presentations is beyond the scope of this book. For more information on how to record sounds, consult your WP Presentations reference manual and the Windows 3.1 User Guide.

WP Presentations also allows you to play music from your PC CD-ROM player. If you want to add all or part of a favorite song to a slide, you can put the CD in your PC's CD-ROM player and add the song to the slide show.

Adding MIDI or Digital Sound

When you add MIDI or digital sound to a slide show, you are telling WP Presentations to link or associate a sound file to a specific slide in the slide show. When you play the slide show and display those slides, WP Presentations will open the sound files and play the music, voice, or special effects over your PC speakers. To add sound files to your slides, follow these steps:

1. Open an existing slide show or create a new one.

2. Open the Slide menu and click on Sound. The Sound dialog box appears (see Figure 21.1).

3. Click on the slide arrow buttons to select the slide that you want to add sound to.

Click these arrows to select the slide
that you want to add sound to.

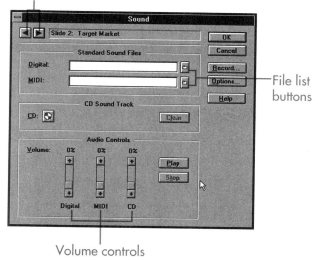

Volume controls

Figure 21.1 Adding sound files to slides.

4. If you want to use a Digital sound file, enter the
directory and file name in the Digital file name box,
or click on the Digital list button to display the
Select File dialog box, as shown in Figure 21.2. You
can use that dialog box, much as you would the File
Open dialog box, to select the directory and file
name of the sound file you want to use. You can
find the digital sound files that come with WP
Presentations in the c:\prwin\sound subdirectory.
These files have a .WAV extension, as is the case
with most digital sound files (they are often called
sound wave files).

Default Sound Directory The default
directory for sound clip files is the subdirectory
named c:\prwin\sound. To change the default
directory, use File Preferences and double-click on
Locations of Files. In the Sound Clips text box, specify the
new sound directory and click on the OK button.

5. If you want to use a MIDI file, follow the same procedure as outlined in step 4. You can click on the MIDI list button to display the Select File dialog box and select the directory and filename for the MIDI files. The MIDI files that come with WP Presentations have a .MID extension and, by default, are located in the c:\prwin\sound subdirectory.

Specify sound filename by entering it here or by clicking on it in the Files list box.

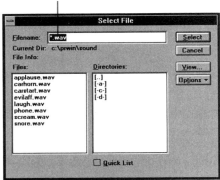

Figure 21.2 Select File dialog box.

6. In the Audio Controls group box, drag the volume controls to choose the volume level of the sound that you are adding to the slide; 0% means there is no sound and 100% is as loud as the sound will play. Make sure you adjust the volume control for the type of file you are adding.

7. When you have set the volume, click on the Play button to test the sound. Adjust the volume control button until the sound is at the right volume for you.

8. Click on the OK button. You return to your slide show. When you play the slide show, you should hear the sounds you have chosen for your slides.

Adding CD Audio Sound

You may have music on your stereo compact discs that you want to play as background music during your slide show. When you add CD sound to your slide show, you are instructing WP Presentations to play all or part of a song (track) on the CD while a particular slide appears. WP Presentations does not create and store CD audio sounds in sound files, such as MIDI and digital sounds. WP Presentations plays a CD track directly from the CD, which you insert into the CD-ROM player of your PC. That particular CD must be in the CD-ROM player every time you play the show. To add sound from a CD, follow these steps:

1. Open an existing slide show or create a new one.

2. Put the CD in your PC's CD-ROM player.

3. Open the Slide menu and click on Sound.

4. Click on the slide arrow buttons to select the slide that you want to add sound to.

5. Click on the CD button. The Slide CD-Audio dialog box appears (see Figure 21.3).

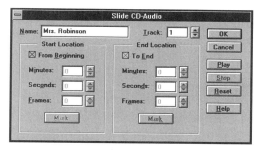

Figure 21.3 Adding CD sound to a slide show.

6. In the Name text box, type a descriptive name for the sound clip.

7. In the Track number box, enter the sound track number. This is the number of the song on the CD.

8. If you want to play the entire musical piece from the beginning to the end of the track, select the From Beginning and To End check boxes (an **X** appears in the check boxes). If you don't want to play the entire song, select the length of time you want the music to play by entering the minutes, seconds, and frames for both the Start Location and End Location.

9. If you want to test the sound, click on the Play button.

10. Click on the OK button. The Sound dialog box appears (see Figure 21.1).

11. Adjust the volume control for the CD. Click on the Play button again to test the volume.

12. If you want to add CD sound to more slides, repeat steps 4 through 10, or click on the OK button. Your slide show appears. When you play your slide show, the CD selection(s) you have chosen will play when the slide appears.

In this chapter, you have learned how to enhance your presentation by adding music and other sounds to your slides. In the next lesson, you will learn how to link spreadsheet and ASCII files to your WP Presentations charts.

Lesson

Linking Charts

In this lesson, you will learn how to link spreadsheets (from other applications) and ASCII files to your slide show.

Linking Basics

As you learned in Lesson 12, if you create spreadsheets or simple databases in other applications, such as Quattro Pro, Lotus 1-2-3, and Excel, you can use the spreadsheet data to create a WP Presentations data chart. That process is called *importing*, which means retrieving all or part of the data from another application file into a WP Presentations slide show.

A more powerful way of sharing data between another application and WP Presentations is by using the *linking* feature. When you link a spreadsheet, graph, or ASCII file to a WP Presentations chart within a slide show, you create an interaction between the spreadsheet file and the WP Presentations file. With a link in place, WP Presentations will automatically update your WP Presentations chart with any changes you make in the spreadsheet data.

If you want to edit the linked data, you must do so in the source spreadsheet file or source graph. You can make changes to the data in the WP Presentations worksheet; however, it will not affect the source data in the linked spreadsheet file.

WP Presentations allows you to link to spreadsheets or graphs. You will learn how to do all of these things in this lesson.

Linking Spreadsheets to a Chart

WP Presentations supports the following spreadsheet programs:

- Quattro Pro for Windows, Quattro, and Quattro Pro (Versions 2.0–4.0 for DOS)

- Lotus 1-2-3 for Windows

- Lotus 1-2-3 (Versions 2.01–3.1 for DOS)

- Microsoft Excel (Versions 2.1–4.0)

- PlanPerfect (Versions 3.0–5.1)

To link a spreadsheet to a WP Presentations chart, follow these steps:

1. Open the Chart Editor by clicking on the Select tool in the tool palette and double-clicking on the chart.

2. Click on the WP Presentations worksheet cell where you want to begin importing the data from the spreadsheet.

3. Open the File menu and click on Import. The Import Chart Data dialog box appears (see Figure 22.1).

> **Shortcut Keys**   While in the Chart Editor, press F4 to import spreadsheet data.

4. Enter the filename of the spreadsheet in the Filename text box.

5. Click on the Import button. The Import Spreadsheet dialog box appears (see Figure 22.2).

Enter path and filename
of spreadsheet here.

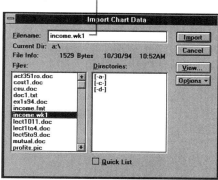

Figure 22.1   Linking a spreadsheet file to a chart.

Figure 22.2   The Import Spreadsheet dialog box.

6. Click on the Link to Spreadsheet check box to select it.

7. Click on the Clear Current Data check box to select it. *Warning: Any existing data in your WP Presentations worksheet will be replaced!*

8. If you only want to link to a range of data in the spreadsheet file, enter the range name in the Range text box, or click on the range name in the Range Name list box. If you want to link to the entire spreadsheet file, select the spreadsheet from the Range Name list box. If you need more information on range names, consult the user guide.

9. If you want to link a graph that was created in a spreadsheet program, click on the name of the graph in the Range Name list box. In many spreadsheet programs, you can name graphs the same way you name ranges of data. The advantage of linking to the graph is that WP Presentations will use the chart attributes (color, title, legend, and so on) that you used in the original spreadsheet graph.

10. Click on the OK button. The imported data appears in the WP Presentations worksheet; if you click on the Redraw button, the new graph also appears. WP Presentations establishes the link but does not save it until you save the WP Presentations file. The next time you open the WP Presentations file, the link will be in effect and updated. This means that WP Presentations updates any chart data that you change in the spreadsheet application in your WP Presentations chart because you have established the link.

11. To save the link, click on the Return button and save the file. (See Lesson 7 for information on saving files.)

Linking ASCII Files

If WP Presentations does not support your spreadsheet software, don't despair. You can still import data from your spreadsheet. Many applications, such as spreadsheets, word processing, and database programs allow you to save data in ASCII format. This is a file format that just about all applications can read. Here are the steps to link your WP Presentations graph to an ASCII file:

1. Open the Chart Editor by clicking on the Select Tool in the Tool palette and double-clicking in the chart.

2. Click on the WP Presentations worksheet cell where you want to begin importing the data from the spreadsheet.

3. Open the File menu and click on Import. The Import Chart Data dialog box appears (see Figure 22.1).

4. Enter the path and the filename of the ASCII file that you want to link to.

5. Click on the Import button. The Text Import dialog box appears (see Figure 22.3).

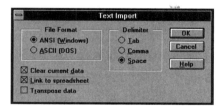

Figure 22.3   Linking an ASCII file to a WP Presentations chart.

6. You may have to select the File Format and the Delimiter, but WP Presentations will make a default choice for you. Try the File Format and Delimiter selections made by WP Presentations. If the data doesn't seem to be correct as it is linked, try again and change the file format and delimiter.

Delimiter Also called *separators*. Spaces, commas, and tabs are examples of delimiters. They separate one piece of data from another in a file.

7. Click on the Clear current data check box. *Warning: Again, any existing data on the WP Presentations worksheet will be overwritten!*

8. Click on the Link to spreadsheet check box so that it is selected.

9. Click on the OK button. The imported data appears in the WP Presentations worksheet, and if you click on the Redraw button, the new graph also appears. You have established the link, but it is not saved until you save the WP Presentations file. The next time you open the WP Presentations file, the link will be updated. This means that WP Presentations will update the chart data that you change in the ASCII file, in your WP Presentations chart because you have established the link.

10. To save the link, click on the Return button and save the file. (See Lesson 7 for information on saving files.)

In this lesson, you learned how to link your spreadsheet files, spreadsheet graphs, and ASCII files to your WP Presentations charts. In Lesson 23, you will learn how to work with Bitmaps to create graphical images and drawings.

Lesson

Working with Bitmaps

In this lesson, you will learn how to open a bitmap file so you can add it to a slide, and how to create and edit bitmap images within your slide show.

Retrieving Bitmaps

Sometimes, clip art and other graphical images, such as scanned images, are created and saved in the Bitmap format. This lesson shows you how to bring those images into your slide show, how to create bitmaps, and how to edit them.

Bitmaps is a generic name given to graphics images that are formed by a series of dots, also called *pixels*. A bitmap image is also sometimes called a *paint image*, because you can create bitmaps with the Windows Paintbrush application. You can find the Windows Paintbrush program in your Windows Accessories window. When you scan photographs and other images with a scanner, the image you create is also often in a bitmap format.

To retrieve a bitmap to include in your slide show, follow these steps:

1. Locate the slide in which you want to retrieve a bitmap. Click on the Figure tool in the tool palette.

2. Move the mouse to the area of the slide where you want the bitmap to be inserted. Click and drag the mouse pointer across the slide window to create a rectangular area, or click once to have the bitmap cover the entire slide.

3. Release the mouse button. The Figure Gallery dialog box appears.

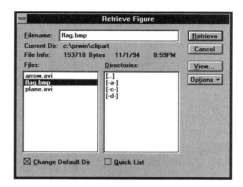

Figure 23.1   The Retrieve Figure dialog box.

4. Click on the Other File button. The Retrieve Figure dialog box appears.

5. Select a drive, directory, and enter a filename. To learn how to select a drive and directory, see Lesson 7. Filenames with the extensions such as bmp, PCX, and TIF are bitmaps.

6. Click on the Retrieve button. WP Presentations inserts the bitmap image in the rectangular shape area on your slide. The bitmap figure is automatically sized to fill the defined area.

Creating Bitmaps

You can create (draw) your own bitmap images by using the Bitmap tools in WP Presentations. Creating good-looking bitmaps takes some practice. Drawing with a mouse can be quite cumbersome, especially at first. WP Presentations does have a palette of Bitmap tools that is available when you are in the Bitmap Editor window (an area in which you can create and edit graphics). These tools can help you to create the image. They also are helpful when editing an image, which is the topic of the last section of this lesson.

1. Click on the Bitmap tool in the Tool palette, or select Bitmap from the Draw menu.

2. Click and drag to create an area large enough for the bitmap graphic, or click once to create a full page figure. You are now in the Bitmap Editor window.

3. Use the tools on the Bitmap Tool palette to create a bitmap image. The bitmap tools are shown in Figure 23.2. For information on the drawing tools in the palette (shapes, lines, and so on) see Lessons 14 and 15, which discuss how to draw and enhance shapes.

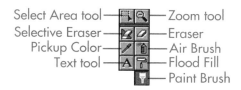

Select Area tool — Zoom tool
Selective Eraser — Eraser
Pickup Color — Air Brush
Text tool — Flood Fill
Paint Brush

Figure 23.2 The Bitmap editing tools.

Paint Tool	What It Does
Select Area tool	Selects an area within a bitmap so that you can cut, copy, or erase.
Zoom tool	Expands or reduces the bitmap image on screen but does not change its actual size.
Eraser	Erases all pixels that it touches.
Selective Eraser	Erases only selective colors.
Air Brush	Randomly creates colored pixels as you drag.

continues

Continued

Paint Tool	What It Does
Flood Fill	Fills an area with a color.
Paint Brush	Fills a pixel square with color when you click, and fills all pixel squares that it touches as you drag.
Pickup Color	Captures a color from a bitmap image to use as a foreground or background fill color.

Bitmap images are saved with your slide show when you save the slide show. See Lesson 7 for details on how to save a slide show. However, the image gets converted to what is called a *Vector file* format. Vector-formatted images are not made up of pixels. They are made up of lines, which results in crisper edges around the image instead of the sometimes jagged edges of a bitmap image. If you want to keep a file in the Bitmap format, you must choose the Bitmap, PCX, or TIFF format when you save the file. For details on how to save files in those formats, consult your WP Presentations Reference guide.

Editing Bitmaps

Editing a bitmap involves changing its shape, size, and colors. A bitmap is made of tiny dots called pixels. Therefore, to edit the bitmap, you must edit the pixels. You can do pixel-by-pixel editing in the Bitmap Editor.

Bitmap Editor Another type of WP Presentations window, the Bitmap Editor allows you to make changes to bitmap images.

To edit an existing bitmap, follow these steps:

1. Click on the Select tool in the tool palette and double-click in the bitmap. The Bitmap Editor window opens, and the status bar at the bottom of the screen indicates you are in the Bitmap Editor.

2. To edit the individual pixels, click on the Zoom tool in the Bitmap Editor tool palette. The screen divides into three areas (see Figure 23.3): the Full Bitmap box, the Actual Size box, and the Zoom Editor, which is an enlarged area of the bitmap used for editing each pixel in the bitmap. Use the Full Bitmap and Actual Size boxes to select an area of the bitmap to edit.

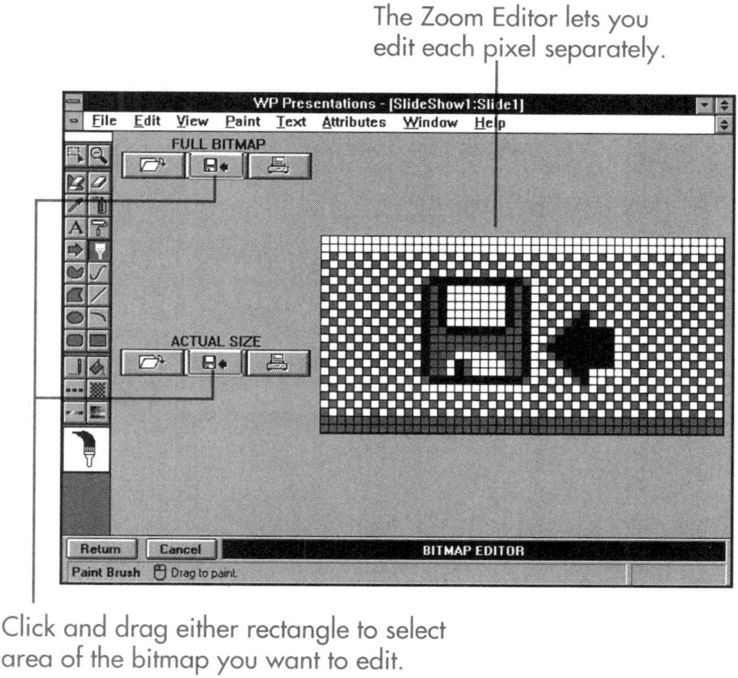

The Zoom Editor lets you edit each pixel separately.

Click and drag either rectangle to select area of the bitmap you want to edit.

Figure 23.3   The Zoom Editor.

3. Drag the rectangle in the Full Bitmap box or the Actual Size box to select the area of the bitmap that you want to edit. As you move the rectangle, your selection is shown in the Zoom Editor.

4. Click on one of the Paint tools from the tool palette to edit the bitmap colors and patterns. You can also erase or color pixels. For example, if you want to color some pixels, click on the Paintbrush tool, choose a color using the Fill Color palette tool, and click on individual pixels or drag the mouse pointer across the pixels. For more information on how to choose colors from the Fill Color palette, see Lesson 15.

5. To exit the Zoom Editor, click on the Return button. You are returned to the slide show drawing window.

6. To change the size of a bitmap, while in the slide window (also called the drawing window), click on the Select tool, and click on the bitmap to display the eight handles that surround it. Move the mouse over one of the handles until the pointer becomes a double-headed arrow. Click and drag the handle to shrink or expand the bitmap.

In this lesson, you learned to retrieve, create, and edit Bitmap files within the WP Presentations slide show.

Appendix

Microsoft Windows Primer

Microsoft Windows is an interface program that makes your computer easier to use by enabling you to select menu items and pictures so you don't have to type commands. Before you can take advantage of it, however, you must learn some Windows basics.

Starting Microsoft Windows

To start Windows, do the following:

1. At the DOS prompt, type win.

2. Press Enter.

The Windows title screen appears for a few moments, and then you see a screen similar to the one in Figure A.1.

What If It Didn't Work? You may have to change to the Windows directory before starting Windows; to do so, type **cd\windows** and press Enter.

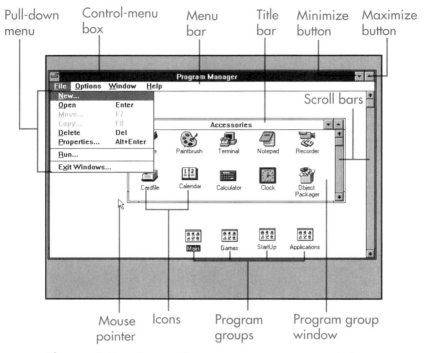

Pull-down menu • Control-menu box • Menu bar • Title bar • Minimize button • Maximize button • Scroll bars • Mouse pointer • Icons • Program groups • Program group window

Figure A.1 The Windows Program Manager with the Accessories group and the File menu selected.

Parts of a Windows Screen

As shown in Figure A.1, the Windows screen contains several unique elements that you won't see in DOS. Here's a brief summary.

* *Title bar*   Shows the name of the window or program.

* *Program group windows*   Contain program icons that allow you to run programs.

* *Icons*   Graphic representations of programs. To run a program, you select its icon.

- *Minimize and Maximize buttons*   Alter a window's size. The Minimize button shrinks the window to the size of an icon. The Maximize button expands the window to fill the screen. When maximized, a window contains a double-arrow *Restore* button, which returns the window to its original size.

- *Control-menu box*   When selected, pulls down a menu that offers size and location controls for the window. Double-click on the Control-menu box to close the currently open window.

- *Pull-down menu bar*   Contains a list of the pull-down menus available in the program.

- *Mouse pointer*   If you are using a mouse, the mouse pointer (usually an arrow) appears on-screen. It can be controlled by moving the mouse (discussed later in this appendix).

- *Scroll bars*   If a window contains more information than it can display, you will see a scroll bar. Clicking on the *scroll arrows* on each end of the scroll bar allows you to scroll slowly. Clicking on the *scroll box* allows you to scroll more quickly.

Using a Mouse

To work most efficiently in Windows, you should use a mouse. You can press mouse buttons and move the mouse in various ways to change the way it acts:

Point means to move the mouse pointer onto the specified item by moving the mouse. The tip of the mouse pointer must be touching the item.

Click on an item means to move the pointer onto the specified item and press the mouse button once. Unless specified otherwise, use the left mouse button.

Double-click on an item means to move the pointer onto the specified item and press and release the left mouse button twice quickly.

Drag means to move the mouse pointer onto the specified item, hold down the mouse button, and move the mouse while holding down the button.

  Figure A.2 shows how to use the mouse to perform common Windows activities, including running applications and moving and resizing windows.

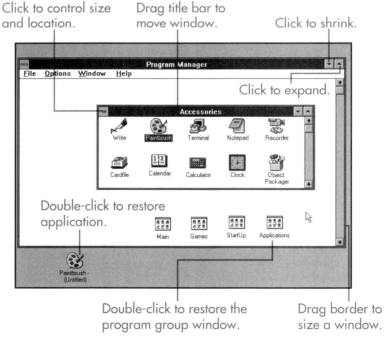

Figure A.2 Use your mouse to control Windows.

Starting a Program

To start a program, simply select its icon. If its icon is in a program group window that's not open at the moment, open the window first. Follow these steps:

1. If necessary, open the program group window that contains the program you want to run. To open a program group window, double-click on its icon.

2. Double-click on the icon for the program you want to run.

Using Menus

The menu bar contains various pull-down menus (see Figure A.3) from which you can select commands. Each Windows program that you run has a set of pull-down menus; Windows itself has a set, too.

To open a menu, click on its name on the menu bar. Once a menu is open, you can select a command from it by clicking on the desired command.

Shortcut Keys Notice that in Figure A.3, some commands are followed by key names such as Enter (for the Open command) or F8 (for the Copy command). These are called *shortcut keys*. You can use these keys to perform the commands without even opening the menu.

Usually, when you select a command, the command is performed immediately. However:

- If the command name is gray (instead of black), the command is unavailable at the moment, and you cannot choose it.

- If there is an arrow after the command name, selecting the command will cause another menu to appear, from which you must select another command.

- If an ellipsis (three dots) follows the command name, selecting the command will cause a dialog box to appear. You'll learn about dialog boxes in the next section.

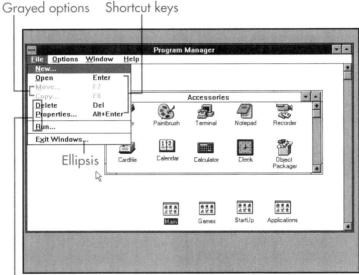

Grayed options   Shortcut keys

Ellipsis

Selection letters

Figure A.3   A pull-down menu lists various commands you can perform.

Navigating Dialog Boxes

A dialog box is Windows' way of requesting additional information. For example, if you choose Print from the File menu of the Write application, you'll see the dialog box shown in Figure A.4.

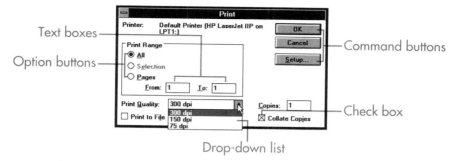

Text boxes

Option buttons

Command buttons

Check box

Drop-down list

Figure A.4 A typical dialog box.

Each dialog box contains one or more of the following elements:

- *List boxes* display available choices. To activate a list, click inside the list box. If the entire list is not visible, use the scroll bar to view the items in the list. To select an item from the list, click on it.

- *Drop-down lists* are similar to list boxes, but only one item in the list is shown. To see the rest of the items, click on the down arrow to the right of the list box. To select an item from the list, click on it.

- *Text boxes* allow you to type an entry. To activate a text box, click inside it. To edit an existing entry, use the arrow keys to move the cursor and the Del or Backspace keys to delete existing characters. Then type your correction.

- *Check boxes* allow you to select one or more items in a group of options. For example, if you are styling text, you can select Bold and Italic to have the text appear in both bold and italic type. Click on a check box to activate it.

- *Option buttons* are like check boxes, but you can select only one option button in a group. Selecting one button unselects any option that is already selected. Click on an option button to activate it.

- *Command buttons* execute (or cancel) the command once you have made your selections in the dialog box. To press a command button, click on it.

Switching Between Windows

Many times, you will have more than one window open at once. Some open windows may be program group windows, while others may be actual programs that are running. To switch among them, you can:

- Pull down the Window menu and choose the window you want to view

  or

- If a portion of the desired window is visible, click on it.

Controlling a Window

As you saw earlier in this appendix, you can minimize, maximize, and restore windows on your screen. You can also move them and change their size.

- To move a window, drag its title bar to a different location. (Remember, *drag* means to hold down the left mouse button while you move the mouse.)

- To resize a window, position the mouse pointer on the border of the window until you see a double-headed arrow; then drag the window border to the desired size.

Copying Your Program Diskettes with File Manager

Before you install any new software, you should make a copy of the original diskettes as a safety precaution. Windows' File Manager makes this process easy.

First, start File Manager by double-clicking on the File Manager icon in the Main program group. Then, for each disk you need to copy, follow these steps:

1. Locate a blank disk of the same type as the original disk and label it to match the original. Make sure the disk you select does not contain any data that you want to keep.

2. Place the original disk in your diskette drive (A or B).

3. Open the Disk menu and select Copy Disk. The Copy Disk dialog box appears.

4. From the Source In list box, select the drive used in step 2.

5. Select the same drive from the Destination In list box. (Don't worry, File Manager will tell you to switch disks at the appropriate time.)

6. Select OK. The Confirm Copy Disk dialog box appears.

7. Select Yes to continue.

8. When you are instructed to insert the Source diskette, choose OK since you already did this in step 2. The Copying Disk box appears, and the copy process begins.

9. When you are instructed to insert the target disk, remove the original disk from the drive and insert the blank disk. Then choose OK to continue. The Copying Disk box disappears when the process is complete.

Index